COOKING WITH
Bon Appétit

COOKING WITH
Bon Appétit

Oriental Favorites

THE KNAPP PRESS
Publishers
Los Angeles

Copyright © 1986 by Knapp Communications Corporation

Published by The Knapp Press
5900 Wilshire Boulevard, Los Angeles, California 90036

Library of Congress Cataloging in Publication Data

Main entry under title:

Oriental favorites.

  (Cooking with Bon appétit)
  Includes index.
  1. Cookery, Oriental. I. Bon appétit. II. Series.
TX724.5.075 1986   641.595   85-31230
ISBN 0-89535-177-3

On the cover: *Kaye's Stir-fried Shrimp and Vegetables*

Printed and bound in the United States of America

10 9 8 7 6 5 4 3

❦ Contents

🍐 *Foreword*

From the high plateaus of northern China to the tropical islands of Indonesia, the foods of the Orient tempt the senses with tantalizing aromas, textures and flavors. With names like Fried Fragrant Bells and Jewel Jellied Chicken Soup, they offer a taste of the exotic and romantic. Often resembling delicate works of art, dishes like Chrysanthemum Sushi with Red Caviar and Vietnamese Fruit Fantasy appeal to the visual senses as well as to the palate.

This collection of more than 200 *Bon Appétit* recipes includes authentic Chinese, Japanese and Southeast Asian dishes that represent the best of Oriental cooking. A glossary and listing of mail-order sources for Asian ingredients, tips for preparing Chinese and Japanese meals, and step-by-step instructions make preparing these delicacies surprisingly easy. From appetizers to desserts, you will find the makings of a casual supper for two or a banquet fit for a mandarin.

For an authentic Asian feast, why not start the meal with a flourish? Lead off with an assortment of Japanese sushi; our easy-to-follow instructions make it simple to prepare this treat at home. Or sample elegant Shrimp Nuggets with Orange Plum Sauce or creamy Chicken and Shrimp Steamed in Custard. Novel entrées such as Grilled Duck in Coconut Milk, Stir-fried Lobster with Ginger and Peking Sesame Beef will make a hit at any gathering. Accompany them with a rice or noodle dish such as Mee Krob or Hué Rice, add a side dish of Vegetarian Ten Mix or Malaysian Spinach Salad with Spicy Dressing, and finish up with Chilled Almond Ivory for an exquisite taste of the Orient.

But you don't need to prepare a full Oriental menu in order to enjoy these recipes. Incorporate them into your everyday meals for an exciting change. Serve Crisp Vegetable Egg Rolls or Chicken Satés and Ginger-Peanut Sauce at your next dinner party. Or a hearty bowl of Chinese Chicken-Corn Soup and Rice Noodle Salad with Chinese Sausage, Eggplant and Basil for an unusual luncheon. Japanese Double-fried Chicken with Ginger and Sesame Oil and Tea Eggs are perfect for any picnic.

Even the all-American barbecue is a great place to serve favorites like Korean Grilled Short Ribs or Orange Barbecued Spareribs.

These Oriental recipes from *Bon Appétit* will introduce you to a delicious world of colorful and unusual dishes that you will want to share with your family and friends.

1 ❧ Appetizers

A well-selected appetizer should provide a tantalizing hint of the dishes to follow and also make a distinct impression of its own. Oriental appetizers do both admirably, offering exciting flavors, unique textural blends and looks that can approach sheer artistry.

With their thousands of miles of coastline, the Asian countries make the most of fresh seafood. Japanese *sashimi* (sliced raw fish) is always served as an appetizer so that it can be fully enjoyed before other flavors intervene. Sashimi with Dipping Sauces (page 8), attractively arranged on a decorative platter, will be the highlight of any Japanese-style meal. In the port city of Shanghai, Soy-smoked Fish (page 9) is popular at cold buffets—in part because busy cooks know that the intriguing smoky flavor is enhanced when the dish is prepared ahead of time.

Rolled appetizers appear in various forms throughout the Orient. Japanese *sushi* (page 7) combines tangy vinegared rice with the freshest strips of raw seafood, garnished with a touch of fiery green horseradish and perhaps a bit of vegetable or omelet. Traditional at Filipino family gatherings, Shrimp Lumpia (page 11) calls for delicate wrappers filled with slivered fresh vegetables and shrimp. Thai Pork and Crabmeat Rolls (page 20) are a snappy finger food dipped in a sweet and sour vinegar-garlic sauce. And how could we forget Crisp Vegetable Egg Rolls (page 2)? Filled with crunchy vegetables, with cilantro and peanuts added for an element of surprise, these rolls are fried until golden, then served on ribbons of lettuce.

For visual delight, few appetizers can beat Tea Eggs (page 12): Hard-cooked eggs are tapped to crack the shells, then marinated in soy sauce and tea to develop a distinctive marble pattern. Also egg-based but altogether different is Indonesia's Bali Eggs (page 13), an eyecatching brunch dish in which hard-cooked eggs are simmered in a spicy red sauce.

Oriental appetizers add a touch of versatility to every cook's repertoire: A single selection served as a sit-down first course sets the tone for an exciting meal, while a buffet table featuring an array of hot and cold appetizers is an easy but impressive way to celebrate special occasions.

Vietnamese Vegetable Platter (Dia Rau Song)

Raw vegetables are an important part of every Vietnamese meal.

Boston or Bibb lettuce leaves
Fresh mint leaves

Cilantro leaves
Cucumber

Mound lettuce in center of platter. Arrange mint and cilantro leaves in separate groups along sides. Remove cucumber peel in alternating strips. Halve cucumber lengthwise, then slice thinly crosswise. Arrange in overlapping pattern around edges of platter.

Crisp Vegetable Egg Rolls

Makes 12

½ ounce dried shiitake mushrooms

14 ounces green cabbage, cored and cut into wedges to fit processor feed tube

2 quarts salted water

¼ cup dry-roasted peanuts
2 large garlic cloves
1 1-inch piece peeled fresh ginger
4 ounces mushrooms, quartered
2 tablespoons peanut oil
1 8-ounce can water chestnuts, drained

12 green onions, trimmed and cut into processor feed tube lengths
2 cups bean sprouts

½ cup cilantro leaves
2 tablespoons oyster sauce
1 tablespoon dry Sherry
1 tablespoon soy sauce
½ teaspoon dried red pepper flakes
¼ teaspoon salt

12 egg roll wrappers

1 quart peanut oil
1 tablespoon oriental sesame oil

1 large head Boston lettuce, thinly sliced
¼ cup cilantro leaves
Ginger-Mustard Dipping Sauce*

Soak shiitake mushrooms in enough warm water to cover until soft, about 30 minutes. Squeeze dry. Cut out stems and discard. Thinly slice caps. (Soaking liquid can be reserved for soups or sauces.) Set aside.

Arrange cabbage wedges cut side down in processor feed tube and slice using firm pressure with medium slicer. Cook in 2 quarts boiling salted water 30 seconds. Drain and rinse under cold water to cool completely. Wrap in towel and squeeze out as much moisture as possible (repeat with another towel if necessary). Transfer cabbage to large bowl.

Insert steel knife into processor. Coarsely chop peanuts; set aside. With machine running, drop garlic and ginger through feed tube and mince finely. Add mushrooms and chop finely using on/off turns. Heat 2 tablespoons peanut oil in heavy 8-inch skillet over medium-low heat. Add mushroom mixture and cook until mushrooms are soft and most of liquid has evaporated, stirring often, about 10 minutes. Add to cabbage. Finely chop water chestnuts in processor using on/off turns. Add to cabbage.

Insert thin slicer. Arrange green onions horizontally in processor feed tube and slice into long slivers using light pressure. Add to cabbage with shiitake, bean sprouts, ½ cup cilantro leaves, oyster sauce, Sherry, soy sauce, dried red pepper flakes and salt. Toss to combine.

Arrange 1 egg roll wrapper diagonally on work surface. Place ½ cup cabbage mixture in compact strip across lower middle of wrapper. Fold bottom flap up over filling, then fold in 2 side flaps. Brush upper point lightly with water, then roll up tightly, pressing gently to seal. Repeat with remaining egg roll wrappers and filling.

Heat 1 quart peanut oil with sesame oil in 2½-quart saucepan or deep fryer to 350°F. Fry 3 egg rolls until golden brown, turning occasionally, about 2 minutes. Drain on paper towels. Reheat oil to 350°F. Continue cooking remaining egg rolls in 3 batches. (*Egg rolls can be cooled completely, wrapped in paper towels and refrigerated up to 2 days, or wrapped in 2 plastic bags and frozen up to 3 months. Thaw frozen rolls in refrigerator. Refry egg rolls as above, or arrange on baking sheet in cold oven, turn temperature to 500°F and bake 10 minutes.*)

Arrange lettuce on platter. Cut egg rolls diagonally into 3 slices. Arrange atop lettuce. Sprinkle with reserved peanuts and cilantro leaves. Drizzle some of dipping sauce over each. Serve immediately, with remaining sauce.

*Ginger-Mustard Dipping Sauce

Makes about ⅔ cup

2 1-inch pieces peeled fresh ginger
2 garlic cloves
¼ cup sugar
3 tablespoons soy sauce
2 tablespoons distilled white vinegar

2 tablespoons catsup
2 tablespoons water
1 teaspoon dry mustard
¼ teaspoon oriental sesame oil

With machine running, drop ginger and garlic through processor feed tube and mince finely. Add remaining ingredients and blend 30 seconds, stopping once to scrape down sides of work bowl. Transfer dipping sauce to small bowl.

Can be made 1 day ahead. Cover tightly and refrigerate.

Green Onion Pancakes

6 servings

2 cups unbleached all purpose flour
⅔ cup boiling water

2 tablespoons oriental sesame oil
4 green onions (including

tops), minced
Pinch of salt

8 tablespoons (about) vegetable oil

Combine flour and boiling water in processor and mix until dough is soft and elastic, about 45 seconds (or knead by hand about 10 minutes). Cover with kitchen towel and let stand 20 minutes to several hours.

Transfer dough to lightly floured work surface and divide into 12 equal pieces. Roll out each piece until very thin. Brush each pancake lightly with sesame oil, then evenly sprinkle each with green onion and salt. Roll pieces up jelly roll fashion, tucking in ends. Roll each out into long, narrow rectangle. Starting at narrow end, roll each up and shape into ball. Roll each ball into round, thin pancake. Cover with towel to retain moisture. Let stand 15 minutes to 1 hour.

Heat 3 tablespoons oil in medium skillet over medium-high heat until very hot but not smoking. Cook pancakes one at a time until blistered and crisp, about 1 minute per side; add more oil to skillet as necessary and discard any browned bits in bottom. Drain on paper towels and keep warm in 200°F oven. Transfer pancakes to heated platter and serve.

Chrysanthemum Sushi with Red Caviar (Kiku-Zushi)

Makes 15 sushi

3½ tablespoons sushi su (seasoned rice vinegar)
2 cups freshly cooked short-grain rice

½ sheet asakusa nori (dried seaweed or laver)

1 tablespoon white sesame seeds

2 tablespoons amazu shōga (pink pickled ginger), drained and chopped

6 to 8 eggs
3 tablespoons dashi* or water
1 tablespoon sugar
1 tablespoon saké

Vegetable oil

⅓ cup red caviar

Sprinkle vinegar over warm rice and toss, fanning rice with piece of stiff cardboard to prevent condensation. Cover with damp cloth and set aside.

Preheat oven to 250°F. Place ½ sheet of laver on baking sheet. Let dry in oven 3 to 4 minutes (or move back and forth over medium-low heat 20 seconds). Wrap in cloth and crumble.

Toast sesame seeds about 1 minute in heavy (thoroughly dry) skillet over medium-high heat, shaking skillet gently in circular motion for even browning. Remove from heat.

Add crumbled laver, sesame seeds and chopped ginger to rice and toss lightly. Dampen hands in acidulated water (to prevent rice from sticking). Divide rice mixture evenly and shape into 15 balls. Place 1 ball in center of damp towel. Gather up ends and twist towel snugly around rice to firm. Repeat with remaining rice balls. Transfer to large serving platter, spacing 1 inch apart. Dampen hands in acidulated water. Flatten each rice ball slightly. Cover with damp cloth and set aside.

Combine eggs, stock, sugar and rice wine in large bowl and beat well. Let batter stand several minutes to allow any foam on top to settle.

Lightly oil 6-inch skillet or crepe pan. Add about 3 to 4 tablespoons batter to pan. Place over medium heat and cook until edges are dry, about 1½ minutes. Turn omelet over and continue cooking until underside is dry, about 30 seconds. Transfer to platter. Repeat with remaining batter, stacking omelets between sheets of waxed paper. Cool completely. Cut into ⅛-inch julienne 3 to 4 inches long.

Lay ribbons of omelet over each rice ball to form "petals" of chrysanthemum. Make indentation in center of each ball and carefully fill with ⅓ to ½ teaspoon red caviar.

*Dashi (Basic Stock)

This clear, light broth, traditionally used as a soup base, gives Japanese food its distinctive flavor.

Makes about 1 quart

5 to 6 inches dashi-konbu (dried kelp)
4½ cups cold water

⅓ cup loosely packed katsuo bushi (dried bonito flakes)

Bring kelp and water to boil in large saucepan over high heat. Immediately remove from heat and sprinkle with dried bonito flakes. Let flakes settle to bottom of saucepan (stir if they do not readily settle). Line colander with linen napkin, towel or handkerchief and set over bowl. Strain stock through cloth, twisting and squeezing to release all liquid.

Dashi can be prepared ahead and refrigerated up to 4 days. Do not freeze.

Japanese Kelp Rolls with Gourd Ribbon (Konbu Maki)

Serve these licorice-like tidbits chilled or at room temperature.

Makes 8 to 10 rolls

4 to 5 feet kanpyō (dried gourd ribbon)

12 inches konbu (dried kelp)

2 cups cold water
2 teaspoons rice vinegar

1 cup dashi (basic stock; see page 4) or water

2 tablespoons saké
1½ tablespoons sugar
3 tablespoons soy sauce
1 tablespoon mirin (syrupy rice wine)

Combine dried gourd in bowl with enough warm water to cover and let soak about 10 minutes. Squeeze gourd between hands using back-and-forth motion. Rinse in cold water and drain well. Return to bowl. Cover with cold water and let soak 5 to 10 minutes. Squeeze gourd using back-and-forth motion. Drain well and pat dry.

Cut kelp in 8 or 10 rectangles. Roll each tightly. Tie some of gourd ribbon around middle of each (use double knot) to resemble scroll. Cut all but 1 inch off each end of gourd ribbon.

Combine 1 cup cold water and 1 teaspoon vinegar in large saucepan and bring to boil over medium-high heat. Add rolls, reduce heat and simmer 5 minutes, skimming any foam that accumulates on surface. Drain well. Repeat process with remaining cold water and vinegar. Drain well.

Rinse saucepan and pat dry. Add dashi and saké and mix well. Add rolls. Place over low heat and cook 5 to 6 minutes. Add sugar and cook another 5 minutes. Stir in soy sauce and cook 5 minutes. Blend in mirin. Increase heat to high and swirl liquid in pan to glaze rolls. Let cool to room temperature, swirling pan several times. Transfer rolls to serving platter.

Maki Sushi

Makes 3 rolls (24 to 30 slices)

½ ounce dried shiitake mushrooms
1 tablespoon sugar
1 tablespoon soy sauce

3 cups cooked short-grain rice
⅓ cup rice vinegar
1½ tablespoons sugar

¾ ounce kanpyō (dried gourd ribbon)
1 tablespoon sugar
1 tablespoon soy sauce

2 eggs
1 tablespoon sugar

1½ teaspoons saké
⅛ teaspoon salt

2 ounces spinach leaves
2 tablespoons water
⅛ teaspoon salt

1/10 ounce (½ of 1/5-ounce package) sukaura denbu (dried fish)

3 seaweed wrappers

¼ cup rice vinegar

Soak mushrooms in small saucepan with water to cover 30 minutes (or overnight). Drain, rinse and cover with fresh water. Add sugar and soy sauce. Bring to boil, then reduce heat and simmer until mushrooms are tender. Drain and let cool. Cut into ½-inch strips and arrange on plate.

Combine rice, vinegar and sugar in bowl and stir lightly until well blended.

Soak kanpyō in small saucepan with water to cover for 5 minutes. Drain, rinse and cover with fresh water. Add sugar and soy sauce. Bring to boil, then reduce heat and simmer until kanpyō are tender. Drain and let cool. Cut lengthwise into ½-inch strips. Arrange on plate alongside mushrooms.

Beat eggs, sugar, saké and salt. Lightly grease small square frying pan or baking pan (preferably 7 inches or less) and place over medium heat. Add egg mixture and let stand until bottom is set; turn in one piece and let cook until second side is set. Cut into ½-inch slices and arrange on plate with sliced mushrooms and kanpyō.

Combine spinach, water and salt in pan and cook gently just until wilted. Drain well. Add to other ingredients.

Place dried fish in small bowl.

Hold seaweed wrappers one at a time about 2 inches above low flame (or medium-high heat of electric range) and move back and forth until wrappers turn burnished green.

Pour rice vinegar into small bowl and place near counter next to sushi mat (sudaré), or use double thickness of aluminum foil cut 2 inches wider than seaweed wrapper. Place sushi mat (or foil) on clean flat surface with slats parallel to working side of table. Lay 1 wrapper on mat. Place 1 cup rice in center. Moisten hands with vinegar to prevent sticking and pat rice in even layer about ½ inch thick, leaving border about 1 inch wide at furthest edge of wrapper.

Divide mushrooms, kanpyō, eggs and spinach into thirds. On closest edge of wrapper place ⅓ of mushrooms in thin strip. Next to mushrooms place ⅓ of kanpyō, then ⅓ egg and ⅓ spinach. Sprinkle ⅓ of dried fish in another line.

Grasping closest edge of mat, roll both wrapper and mat together until wrapper overlaps layer of fish. Press down hard, then release mat but hold beneath wrapper and continue to roll tightly forming a firm cylinder. While sushi is still in mat, rub fingers lightly over entire wrapper to eliminate any bumps. Wrap in waxed paper to prevent drying while making remaining sushi.

To serve, unwrap sushi and cut crosswise into 8 to 10 slices per roll. Arrange cut side down in single layer on plate.

Rolled Sushi with Gourd or Cucumber (Maki Mono)

Makes 8 rolls or 48 bite-size pieces

45 to 50 inches kanpyō (dried gourd ribbon)

½ cup (or more) dashi (basic stock; see page 4)
2 tablespoons soy sauce
2 tablespoons sugar
1½ teaspoons mirin (syrupy rice wine)

3½ tablespoons sushi su (seasoned rice vinegar)
2 cups warm freshly cooked short-grain rice

4 sheets asakusa nori (dried seaweed or laver)

1½ teaspoons white sesame seeds

½ teaspoon wasabi (Japanese green horseradish) paste*
1 thin hothouse cucumber, peeled, halved, seeded and cut into julienne

Soy sauce

Combine dried gourd in bowl with enough warm water to cover and let soak about 20 minutes. Squeeze gourd between hands using back-and-forth motion. Rinse in cold water. Drain well and pat dry.

Combine ½ cup stock, soy sauce, sugar, mirin and gourd in medium saucepan over low heat. Cook 15 minutes, adding more stock if necessary. Remove from heat; let gourd cool in cooking liquid. Cut into 6-inch lengths and set aside.

Sprinkle vinegar over warm rice and toss, fanning rice with piece of stiff cardboard to prevent condensation. Dampen hands in acidulated water (to prevent rice from sticking). Divide rice mixture evenly and shape into 8 balls. Cover with damp cloth and set aside.

Preheat oven to 250°F. Arrange 4 sheets of nori on baking sheet. Let dry in oven 3 to 4 minutes (or move back and forth over medium-low heat one at a time for about 20 seconds). Cut each dried sheet in half.

Open slatted sushi mat (sudaré) on work surface. Place piece of laver on top. Dampen hands and spread 1 rice ball over laver. Arrange 2 gourd strips over rice. Flip edge of mat over filling and press down lightly. Roll up sushi using mat as aid. Remove sushi from mat and set seam side down. Repeat 3 times for a total of 4 gourd sushi.

Toast sesame seeds about 1 minute in heavy, thoroughly dry skillet over medium-high heat, shaking skillet gently in circular motion for even browning. Remove from heat.

Place another piece of nori on slatted mat. Dampen hands and spread 1 rice ball over nori. Paint strip of some of horseradish across middle of rice. Top with some cucumber strips and sprinkle with sesame seed. Roll up as for gourd sushi. Repeat with remaining ingredients for 4 cucumber sushi.

Cut each sushi roll into 6 pieces, wiping knife with damp towel before and after each cut. Arrange on large platter. Serve with soy sauce for dipping.

*If only wasabi powder is available, mix equal parts of powder and water to form paste.

Sushi

Though sushi bars are springing up all over this country, you might like to know how to make your own. To shape the rolls you will need a bamboo place mat or a special reed mat, called a sudaré, *available at stores that sell oriental cooking equipment.*

Makes 12 to 18 slices

Sushi Rice
2 cups Japanese or other short-grain rice
2 cups water
½ cup rice vinegar
6 tablespoons sugar
1 tablespoon salt
1 slice peeled fresh ginger

Wrapping
2 sheets nori (dried seaweed or laver), about 8 × 7 inches each
or
6 eggs
3 tablespoons sugar
2 tablespoons water
¾ teaspoon salt
Vegetable oil

Filling
1 carrot, cut into long, thin strips
1 tablespoon chicken stock or water

1½ teaspoons sugar
1 teaspoon rice vinegar
Salt

3 to 4 green beans

1 ounce large dried mushrooms (preferably shiitake), softened 30 minutes in warm water to cover, drained and cut into strips
1 tablespoon sugar
1 tablespoon Japanese soy sauce
1 tablespoon water
½ teaspoon salt

Wasabi paste (optional; see page 9)

4 to 5 ounces cooked crabmeat or 4 ounces uncooked fresh scallops, thinly sliced
Fresh lemon juice

For rice: Place rice in heavy large saucepan. Add water and let stand 30 minutes to 1 hour. Cover, place over high heat and bring to boil. Without lifting lid, reduce heat to low and cook 12 minutes. Remove from heat and let stand 10 minutes without lifting lid. Meanwhile, combine vinegar, sugar, salt and ginger in small saucepan. Place over medium-low heat until sugar has dissolved, then discard ginger.

Transfer hot rice to large nonmetal platter or tray (rice should cool quickly and metal retains heat). Immediately pour vinegar mixture over top and combine thoroughly with fork, tossing gently so grains of rice remain whole.

For wrapping: If using nori wrapping, check to be sure sheets are shiny and have no holes. Cut sheets in half lengthwise. (Only 3 half-sheets are needed; use remaining piece to patch holes or tears if necessary.) Set aside.

If using egg wrappers, whisk eggs, sugar, water and salt in bowl until well blended. Preheat 8- to 10-inch square skillet or electric frypan to 250°F. Brush bottom lightly with oil. Pour in ½ cup egg mixture and tilt pan in all directions until bottom is evenly coated. Cook until bottom of egg mixture is golden brown, then turn and cook other side. Repeat twice. Drain on paper towels.

For filling: Combine carrot, stock, sugar, vinegar and salt to taste in small saucepan. Cover, place over medium-low heat and simmer until carrot is crisp-tender, about 5 minutes. Cool.

Blanch green beans in pot of boiling salted water until barely tender. Drain and rinse with cold water. Drain well, pat dry and cut into long strips.

Combine mushrooms, sugar, soy sauce, water and salt in small saucepan. Place over low heat and simmer until all liquid has evaporated.

To assemble: Position bamboo mat or sudaré on work surface with bamboo running crosswise. Have bowl of cold water nearby for moistening hands when working with rice. If using nori wrapper, pass each sheet over gas flame to intensify flavor and color. Lay half sheet of nori on mat with long edge of nori at mat edge nearest you. Moisten hands and spread about ¾ cup rice onto wrapper, leaving 1-inch border. If desired, spread lightly with wasabi.

In center of rice arrange line of ⅓ of each of filling ingredients: carrot, green bean, mushroom and crab or scallop. Sprinkle with lemon juice to taste. Holding down filling ingredients with fingers, lift mat with thumbs and use it to help roll up wrapper tightly. Roll until edges of rice meet, pulling away mat as you roll and using gentle pressure to tighten. Press in any ingredients that have escaped ends of roll. Wrap in plastic. Repeat to make 2 more rolls. Chill at least 1 hour before slicing. When thoroughly chilled, cut rolls into slices 1½ inches thick. Arrange slices attractively on platter and serve.

Sashimi with Dipping Sauces

Finding absolutely fresh fish is the only difficulty in preparing sashimi (the Japanese demand that theirs be no more than 12 hours out of the water). If by virtue of geography or uncaring fishmongers you cannot get just-caught fish, substitute another dish; do not attempt to make sashimi with anything less than the best ingredients.

8 appetizer servings

2 pounds boned and skinned fresh ocean fish

1½ cups shredded lettuce
1½ cups shredded daikon (Japanese white radish) or other mild white radish, turnip or cucumber

Mild Dipping Sauce (see recipe)
Spicy Dipping Sauce (see recipe)
Wasabi Paste (see recipe), hot mustard paste or prepared horseradish

Cut away and discard any dark portions of fish. Using very sharp knife, cut fish into slices about ¼ to ½ inch thick and 1 inch wide, or slice into julienne strips (firm fish such as tuna can be cut into ½-inch cubes). Or, cut fish at an angle into almost transparent sheets. Wrap in plastic and chill.

Arrange shredded lettuce along one side of serving platter. Mound radish, turnip or cucumber along opposite side. Lay fish attractively in center. Serve with dipping sauces and wasabi paste, allowing guests to mix sauces and wasabi to their tastes.

Mild Dipping Sauce

Makes about 1¼ cups

1 cup Japanese soy sauce
¼ cup saké or dry Sherry

1 teaspoon finely grated
fresh ginger

Combine soy sauce, saké and ginger in saucepan and bring to boil. Remove from heat and strain into small serving bowl. Serve at room temperature.

Spicy Dipping Sauce

Makes about 1¾ cups

¼ cup saké or dry Sherry
½ cup Japanese soy sauce
½ cup grated daikon (Japanese white radish)

¼ cup rice vinegar or cider vinegar
3 green onions, thinly sliced
¼ teaspoon shichimi tōgarashi (dried blend of hot spices)

Warm saké in small saucepan over medium heat just until heated through. Remove from heat and ignite saké, shaking pan gently until flame subsides. Transfer to small bowl and cool. Add remaining ingredients and mix well. Serve sauce at room temperature.

Wasabi Paste

If wasabi is unavailable, substitute paste made of 2 tablespoons dry mustard mixed with 4 teaspoons water.

Makes about 2 tablespoons

2 tablespoons wasabi (Japanese green horseradish) powder

2 tablespoons water

Blend wasabi powder and water until smooth. Let stand about 5 minutes.

Soy-smoked Fish

Although fried and then simmered, this chewy Shanghainese appetizer has the flavor of smoked fish. It is glazed with an alluring deep-flavored sauce.

2 to 6 appetizer servings

10 ounces ¾-inch-thick lingcod or red snapper steaks
Oil for deep frying

1¼ cups water
4½ tablespoons sugar
3½ tablespoons dark soy sauce

1 tablespoon distilled white vinegar
1 garlic clove, crushed
1 teaspoon five-spice powder

Green onion slivers

Halve fish along bone; do not remove bone. Heat oil in wok or large saucepan to 350°F. Add fish and cook 10 minutes, adjusting heat to maintain oil at 300°F. Turn fish over using spatula. Fry until golden brown, about 5 minutes. Drain on paper towels.

Meanwhile, heat water, sugar, soy sauce, vinegar, garlic and five-spice powder in heavy medium saucepan over low heat, swirling pan occasionally, until sugar dissolves. Increase heat to medium-high and cook until sauce is syrupy, stirring occasionally, about 15 more minutes.

Add fish to sauce and cook over medium heat until sauce coats fish, turning once, about 7 minutes. Cool to room temperature. Refrigerate fish with sauce at least 2 hours. (*Smoked fish can be prepared 2 days ahead.*)

Cut fish into bite-size pieces. Arrange on platter. Spoon sauce over. Garnish with green onions. Let stand for 20 minutes before serving.

Japanese Saké-cooked Clams (Hamaguri Sakani)

6 servings

18 fresh clams in the shell

⅓ cup saké or dry Sherry

Fern fronds or leaves (garnish)
Lemon slices

Shuck clams, discarding shallow half of shell but reserving deeper half. Clean shells thoroughly by dropping into large pot of boiling water. Rinse under cold running water while scrubbing off any remaining sand. Pat dry.

Warm saké in deep saucepan over medium-high heat. When saké is hot, add clams and stir gently. Cover and cook 3 to 4 minutes. Return clams to shells using slotted spoon. Let cool. Line serving platter or flat lacquer box or basket with fern fronds or leaves. Arrange clams on top. Garnish with lemon.

Indonesian Corn Fritters with Crabmeat (Perkedel Jagung)

Makes about 15

1 12-ounce can corn kernels,
well drained
½ cup flaked cooked crabmeat
2 medium shallots, thinly sliced
2 eggs, beaten to blend

2 green onions, thinly sliced
1 tablespoon cornstarch
½ teaspoon salt
¼ teaspoon freshly ground pepper
¼ cup peanut or corn oil

Combine corn, crabmeat, shallot, eggs, green onions, cornstarch, salt and pepper in medium bowl and blend well. Heat oil in wok or heavy large skillet over medium-high heat. Drop 1 heaping tablespoon corn mixture into oil, flattening into oblong shape using back of spoon, and brown on both sides, about 3 minutes. Remove with slotted spoon and drain on paper towel. Repeat with remaining corn mixture. Transfer to platter and serve.

Shrimp Toast

Makes 48 appetizers

Vegetable oil
1 pound uncooked shrimp, peeled
and deveined
¼ cup whole water chestnuts
2 green onions (white part only)
1½ teaspoons dry white wine

1 teaspoon vegetable oil
½ teaspoon salt
½ teaspoon freshly ground pepper

12 slices sandwich bread,
crusts trimmed

Pour oil into deep fryer or skillet to depth of 2 inches and heat to 350°F. Grind shrimp, water chestnuts and onion in processor or grinder until very fine. Add wine, 1 teaspoon vegetable oil, salt and pepper and mix well.

Spread mixture evenly over bread slices. Fry bread in batches until golden brown, about 5 minutes; drain on paper towels. Cut each slice into 4 strips and serve immediately.

Shrimp Nuggets with Orange Plum Sauce

For extra crisp nuggets, refry in hot oil until dark brown. Drain again on paper towels.

6 to 8 servings (about 32 nuggets)

2½ dozen frozen shelled shrimp, thawed and patted dry
1 8-ounce can whole water chestnuts, drained
1 small garlic clove
1 ¼-inch slice fresh ginger, peeled
½ cup fresh parsley leaves
2 large green onions (1 ounce total), cut into 1-inch lengths
2 tablespoons cornstarch
1 tablespoon oyster sauce

1 tablespoon dry Sherry
1 egg white
1 teaspoon oriental sesame oil
½ teaspoon salt
¼ teaspoon sugar

¼ cup cornstarch
¼ cup all purpose flour
Peanut oil for deep frying
Orange Plum Sauce*

Mince shrimp in processor (do not puree) using on/off turns. Transfer to 1-quart mixing bowl. Add water chestnuts to work bowl and mince using on/off turns. Add to shrimp. Wipe out work bowl with paper towels. Mince garlic and ginger by dropping through feed tube with machine running. Add parsley and onion and mince using on/off turns. Add next 7 ingredients and mix 2 seconds. Scrape bowl with spatula and mix another 5 seconds. Add to shrimp and blend well.

Combine remaining cornstarch with flour in mixing bowl. Pour oil into wok or saucepan to depth of 2 inches and heat to 375°F or until small amount of shrimp mixture sizzles when dropped into oil. Roll scant tablespoonfuls of shrimp in cornstarch-flour mixture and fry in batches of 4 until lightly browned, about 2 minutes; make sure oil is hot before adding more shrimp. Drain on paper towels. Transfer to platter and serve immediately with sauce.

Nuggets can be reheated. Arrange in single layer on baking sheet. Place in oven and turn temperature to 450°F; bake 7 to 10 minutes.

*Orange Plum Sauce

Makes about ¼ cup

¼ cup plum preserves
1 tablespoon cider vinegar
1 tablespoon water
1 teaspoon grated orange peel

½ teaspoon cornstarch
½ teaspoon soy sauce
¼ teaspoon dry mustard

Combine all ingredients in processor and mix well. Transfer to small saucepan and bring to boil over medium-high heat, stirring constantly. Remove from heat and let cool. Cover and chill thoroughly. Stir before serving.

Shrimp Lumpia

2 servings

Filling
3 ounces shrimp, shelled, deveined, cooked and finely chopped
¼ cup bamboo shoots, cut into matchstick julienne
2 tablespoons minced greem onion
1 small carrot, peeled and coarsely grated
1 teaspoon soy sauce
1 medium garlic clove, minced
Salt and freshly ground pepper

Wrappers
1 egg
¼ cup cornstarch
3 tablespoons all purpose flour
Pinch of salt
½ cup water
Vegetable oil

Vegetable oil for deep frying
Soy Dipping Sauce*

For filling: Mix all ingredients in bowl. Refrigerate while preparing wrappers.

For wrappers: Whisk egg in medium bowl until frothy, about 1 minute. Whisk in cornstarch, flour and salt. Whisk in water in slow steady stream. Heat 8-inch crepe pan or heavy skillet over medium-high heat. Brush lightly with oil. Ladle 3 to 4 tablespoons batter into corner of pan, tilting so batter coats bottom. Return excess to bowl. Cook until blistered and opaque, about 1 minute. Turn with spatula or flip and cook second side 15 seconds. Slide wrapper out onto kitchen towel or waxed paper. Repeat with remaining batter.

Place ¼ of filling in bottom of 1 wrapper. Fold left and right sides toward center. Roll up from bottom to form neat rectangular package. Repeat with remaining filling and wrappers.

Heat about 1 inch oil in deep fryer or heavy medium skillet to 360°F. Fry lumpia, seam side down, 2 minutes. Turn and fry until golden brown, about 1 minute. Remove with tongs and drain on paper towels. Serve immediately with dipping sauce.

*Soy Dipping Sauce

Makes about ⅓ cup

¼ cup water	½ teaspoon minced garlic
1 tablespoon sugar	½ teaspoon minced fresh ginger
1 tablespoon soy sauce	Dash of hot pepper sauce
¾ teaspoon cornstarch	

Combine all ingredients in heavy small saucepan over low heat and stir until sugar dissolves. Increase heat to high and bring to boil, stirring constantly. Cook until sauce thickens. Transfer to small bowl. (*Can be prepared 2 to 3 hours ahead and covered.*) Serve dipping sauce at room temperature.

Tea Eggs

The longer the eggs are marinated, the fuller their flavor and deeper brown the beautiful marble pattern.

6 appetizer servings

6 hard-cooked eggs	1 jasmine tea bag
2 tablespoons dark soy sauce	1 whole star anise
2 Earl Grey or Orange Pekoe tea bags	

Crack eggshells by tapping all over with back of spoon; do not peel. Cover eggs with water in small saucepan. Add remaining ingredients. Cover and simmer 1 hour, adding more water if necessary to keep eggs submerged. Remove tea bags and star anise from water. Marinate eggs uncovered in refrigerator at least 3 hours. (*Can be prepared 1 day ahead to this point.*)

Peel eggs. May be served whole, halved with a decorative edge, or cut into medium slices.

Bali Eggs (Telor Bumbu Bali)

The seasoning in this dish is intensified when the eggs are prepared the previous day and gently warmed before serving.

6 servings

2 tablespoons corn oil
6 hard-cooked eggs, peeled and patted dry
1 medium-size red bell pepper, cored, seeded and sliced (1 cup)
3/4 cup water
1/4 cup sliced onion
1 tablespoon fresh lemon juice
1 tablespoon Kecap Manis* (Indonesian sweet soy sauce)

1 teaspoon sliced hot red chili or dried chili flakes
1 teaspoon grated fresh ginger
1 teaspoon sliced garlic (about 2 medium cloves)
1/2 teaspoon sugar
1/2 teaspoon salt

Heat oil in wok or heavy large skillet over medium-high heat. Add eggs and stir until browned on all sides, about 5 minutes. Remove eggs from wok.

Puree remaining ingredients in processor. Pour into wok. Place over low heat and cook until sauce thickens and flavors blend, about 10 minutes. Add eggs and simmer about 10 minutes to allow eggs to absorb flavors; baste eggs occasionally and turn after 5 minutes. (*Can be prepared 1 day ahead to this point and refrigerated. Rewarm sauce and eggs over low heat before continuing.*)

To serve, remove eggs from sauce and halve lengthwise. Pour sauce onto rimmed platter. Arrange egg halves in warm sauce cut side up.

*Kecap Manis (Sweet Soy Sauce)

Kecap Manis is an Indonesian seasoning that moves easily from Asian to American cooking. It can be purchased at Asian food stores but the homemade variety is infinitely superior and can be refrigerated indefinitely.

Makes about 3 cups

1 1/2 cups sugar
2 cups Chinese soy sauce
1/4 cup water
3 to 4 lemongrass stalks (about ten 1-inch pieces) or 1 teaspoon sliced stalks

2 garlic cloves, crushed
2 whole star anise

Melt sugar in medium saucepan over low heat until completely dissolved and light caramel color. Gradually stir in soy sauce, water, lemongrass, garlic and star anise, blending well (mixture will bubble over if ingredients are added too quickly). Bring mixture to boil over low heat, stirring constantly, about 10 minutes. Cool 1 hour. Strain through several layers of cheesecloth into jar with tight-fitting lid. Refrigerate sauce until ready to use.

Crispy Chicken Skins

Similar to pork cracklings, these crisp Filipino appetizers can be served by themselves or with Eggplant Dip (see the following recipe). Save skin from chickens to be cooked for other meals and freeze until ready to use.

12 servings

Skins from 4 chickens
1 cup distilled white vinegar
4 small garlic cloves, pounded to paste in mortar with pestle
1/2 teaspoon crushed

black peppercorns
Salt

Vegetable oil for deep frying

Cut chicken skins into 4-inch squares. Combine remaining ingredients except oil in nonaluminum medium bowl. Mix in skins. Cover and refrigerate overnight, turning occasionally.

Drain skins and pat dry. Heat oil in wok or heavy large skillet to 375°F. Carefully add chicken skins in batches (do not crowd) and cook until crisp, turning several times, about 5 minutes. Drain on paper towels and serve.

Eggplant Dip

Traditionally served with Crispy Chicken Skins, this spicy dip is also good with snow peas or crackers.

12 servings

2 large eggplants (about 1 pound each), halved lengthwise
1 cup minced onion
½ cup distilled white vinegar
2 tablespoons sugar

2 tablespoons soy sauce
2 teaspoons salt
2 medium garlic cloves, pounded to paste in mortar with pestle
Freshly ground pepper

Preheat oven to 400°F. Pierce eggplants several times with fork. Place on baking sheet cut surface down. Bake until soft and peel comes off easily with knife, about 30 minutes. Peel eggplants, then mash pulp with fork in large bowl. Mix in remaining ingredients. Cover and refrigerate at least 1 hour.
Can be prepared 1 day ahead.

Chicken Satés and Ginger-Peanut Sauce

2 servings

1 whole chicken breast, skinned, boned and halved
½ cup water
3 tablespoons soy sauce
1 tablespoon firmly packed dark brown sugar
1 garlic clove, minced

Sauce
1 cup chicken stock

¼ cup shelled, skinned fresh-roasted peanuts
1 tablespoon fresh lemon juice
1 tablespoon minced fresh ginger
¼ teaspoon chili powder
1 garlic clove, minced
Salt

Orange slices
Cilantro sprigs

Soak two 10-inch bamboo skewers in cold water 1 hour.

Cut chicken into long strips. Thread strips on skewers, pushing down firmly. Blend ½ cup water, soy sauce, brown sugar and garlic in shallow pan. Add chicken and marinate for 1 to 3 hours, turning frequently.

For sauce: Mix first 6 ingredients in blender until smooth, about 1 minute. Transfer to saucepan. Simmer until thick enough to coat spoon, stirring constantly, about 10 minutes. Season sauce with salt to taste.

Prepare barbecue grill or preheat broiler. Grill or broil satés 4 inches from heat source until golden brown and cooked through, about 3 minutes per side. Set 1 saté on each plate. Garnish with orange and cilantro. Pass sauce separately for dipping.

Malaysian Chicken Saté with Peanut Sauce

If fresh lemongrass is un-available, use five dried stalks, crumbled, or one teaspoon powdered lemongrass.

8 to 10 appetizer servings

Marinade
- 1 tablespoon dried tamarind *or* fresh lemon juice

- 7 shallots
- 2 garlic cloves
- 1 small fresh red chili, seeded
- 1 tablespoon grated fresh ginger
- 1 fresh lemongrass stalk, peeled and cut into 1-inch pieces, *or* 1 strip lemon peel
- 1/4 cup fresh lime juice
- 1 tablespoon ground coriander
- 1 tablespoon firmly packed brown sugar
- 1 teaspoon turmeric

- 1 teaspoon ground cumin
- 1 teaspoon salt
- 1 teaspoon galangal or laos powder (optional)
- 1/2 teaspoon fennel seeds, finely ground

- 2 pounds boned and skinned chicken breasts, cut into 3/4-inch cubes

- 24 thin bamboo skewers, soaked in cold water 1 hour and drained
  Vegetable oil
  Peanut Sauce*

For marinade: If using tamarind, soak in 1/4 cup warm water 5 minutes. Strain tamarind soaking liquid. Press on pulp to extract as much liquid as possible.

With processor running, drop shallots, garlic and chili through feed tube and mince finely. Add ginger and lemongrass and puree. Add tamarind soaking liquid (or lemon juice), lime juice, coriander, sugar, turmeric, cumin, salt, and fennel. Puree.

Mix chicken and marinade in glass dish. Cover and refrigerate 4 hours.

Prepare barbecue or preheat broiler. Thread chicken onto skewers. Brush both sides of chicken with oil. Grill until just springy to touch, about 2 minutes per side. Serve immediately, passing peanut sauce separately.

---

*Peanut Sauce

Makes about 2 cups

- 8 dried red chilies, seeded and cut into 1/2-inch pieces
- 1 tablespoon dried tamarind *or* fresh lemon juice

- 1 medium onion, chopped
- 1 garlic clove, minced
- 1 fresh lemongrass stalk, peeled and cut into 1-inch pieces, *or* 1 strip lemon peel

- 2 tablespoons peanut oil or coconut oil
- 1 1/2 cups coconut milk
- 1/2 cup chunky peanut butter or ground roasted peanuts
- 1 teaspoon ground cumin
- 1 teaspoon firmly packed brown sugar
  Salt

Cover chilies with boiling water. Let stand 10 minutes. If using tamarind, soak in 1/4 cup warm water 5 minutes.

Strain tamarind, reserving soaking liquid. Press on pulp to extract as much liquid as possible. Discard pulp. Drain chilies, discarding water. Puree chilies, onion, garlic and lemongrass in processor or heavy-duty blender. Heat oil in heavy medium skillet over low heat. Add puree mixture and cook 5 minutes, stirring frequently. Add coconut milk and bring to boil, stirring constantly. Add tamarind soaking liquid (or lemon juice), peanut butter, cumin, sugar and salt. Simmer 3 minutes, stirring frequently. Cool. (*Can be prepared 1 day ahead and refrigerated.*) Serve at room temperature.

Ginger Chicken Wontons

It is hard to believe that a half pound of chicken will fill 60 wontons. But it does, making this recipe an enormous money saver compared to buying wontons from carryout restaurants. These can be deep fried to serve as an appetizer or cooked in chicken stock for wonton soup.

Makes 60 wontons (12 to 15 servings if cooked in stock)

2 large dried shiitake mushrooms

1 large garlic clove
2 thin slices ginger, peeled
1 8-ounce can
  water chestnuts, drained
8 ounces boned and skinned
  uncooked chicken, cut into
  1-inch pieces
2 teaspoons soy sauce

1 teaspoon cornstarch
1 teaspoon dry Sherry
1/2 teaspoon salt
1/2 teaspoon dried red pepper flakes

60 wonton wrappers

Oil for deep frying *or*
3 to 4 quarts chicken stock,
  preferably homemade

Cover dried mushrooms with warm water and let stand until softened, about 30 minutes. Drain, squeeze dry and trim stems (reserve stems and soaking liquid for soup if desired).

With machine running, drop garlic and ginger through processor feed tube and mince finely. Add soaked mushrooms, water chestnuts and chicken and chop finely using 6 to 8 on/off turns. Add soy sauce, cornstarch, Sherry, salt and dried pepper flakes and blend for 5 seconds.

Set 1 wonton wrapper on dry work surface with 1 corner facing you. Place 1 1/2 teaspoons chicken mixture in corner nearest you. Roll up wrapper from this corner, leaving half turn unfinished. Pull left and right corners toward center. Moisten inside of one with water and press into opposite corner to seal. (*Can be prepared 1 day ahead to this point and refrigerated.*)

To deep fry wontons, pour vegetable oil into large saucepan to depth of 3 inches and heat to 350°F. Fry wontons several at a time until golden brown. Drain well on paper towels. Serve hot. To cook wontons in stock, bring chicken stock (about 1 cup per serving) to simmer in large saucepan over medium-high heat. Reduce heat to low, add wontons and cook for 3 to 4 minutes.

Oriental Chicken Wings

Makes 16

1 cup soy sauce
1/3 cup sugar
4 teaspoons vegetable oil
1 1/2 teaspoons ground ginger

1/2 teaspoon five-spice powder
2 bunches green onions,
  thinly sliced
16 chicken wings

Blend soy sauce, sugar, oil, ginger and five-spice powder in large bowl until sugar dissolves. Stir in green onions. Add chicken wings to marinade, turning to coat. Cover chicken and refrigerate overnight.

Preheat oven to 350°F. Drain chicken, reserving marinade. Arrange chicken in 9 × 12-inch baking dish. Bake until golden brown and tender, basting occasionally with marinade, 45 to 50 minutes. Serve hot or chilled.

Japanese "Pinecone" Chicken Patties (Tori No Matsukasa Ni)

Each patty resembles a pinecone, which in Japan represents eternity.

8 to 10 servings

3 medium chicken breasts (about 12 ounces total), skinned, boned and ground
1/2 beaten egg
2 tablespoons all purpose flour
1 teaspoon grated fresh ginger
1/4 teaspoon salt
1/2 cup (about) all purpose flour

1 1/2 cups hot water
3 tablespoons soy sauce
2 tablespoons sugar
1 tablespoon saké

Combine chicken, egg, 2 tablespoons flour, ginger and salt in large bowl and blend well. Divide mixture into 8 to 10 portions (mixture will be soft). Lightly flour hands and form mixture into patties. Coat each patty with some of remaining flour. Dip butter knife into flour and score top of each patty diagonally in criss-cross pattern.

Combine water, soy sauce, sugar and wine in large skillet and bring to boil. Carefully add patties to skillet scored side up. Swirl cooking liquid to cover and glaze tops of patties. Reduce heat and simmer 3 to 4 minutes. Gently turn patties over with spatula. Cook 5 to 6 minutes. Turn again. Increase heat to high, swirling pan again to glaze patties. Cook 2 minutes. Transfer patties to platter. Spoon some of cooking liquid over tops of patties and serve.

Japanese Beef and Green Onion Rolls (Negi Maki)

A skewered hors d'oeuvre symbolizing strength and eternity.

Makes about 20

8 to 10 green onions, trimmed and cut into 2- to 3-inch lengths
8 ounces top sirloin (trimmed of fat), sliced paper thin and cut into eight to ten 5 × 2-inch pieces

1 tablespoon vegetable oil or suet
2 tablespoons soy sauce

1 tablespoon sugar
1 tablespoon saké
1 tablespoon dashi (basic stock; see page 4) or water

1 tablespoon mirin (syrupy rice wine)

Divide green onion pieces evenly into 8 to 10 groups. Roll slice of beef snugly around 1 group of onion. Secure with toothpick or tie with string. Repeat with remaining onion and beef.

Heat oil or suet in heavy large skillet over medium-high heat. Add meat rolls seam side down and sauté about 1 minute. Continue sautéing, shaking pan constantly, until rolls are evenly browned. Reduce heat and add soy sauce, sugar, saké and stock. Cook another 3 minutes. Remove meat using slotted spoon and let cool slightly.

Meanwhile, cook pan juices over medium-high heat until reduced by half. Discard toothpicks or string from rolls. Return rolls to skillet. Add syrupy rice wine and shake pan constantly until well glazed. To serve, cut each roll into 1/2-inch rounds and thread on skewer. Arrange on serving platter.

Cold Beef Shank with Five Spices

This favorite Chinese appetizer can be cooked several days in advance.

6 appetizer servings

1 2-pound boneless whole beef shank, trimmed
2½ cups (or more) water
¼ cup soy sauce
2 tablespoons sweet Sherry
8 whole dried red chilies
2 green onions, cut into 1-inch pieces

2 medium garlic cloves, crushed
2 ⅛-inch-thick slices peeled fresh ginger
1 whole star anise (optional)
2 teaspoons Szechwan peppercorns
1½ teaspoons salt
1½ teaspoons five-spice powder
⅛ teaspoon oriental sesame oil

Cook beef shank in large pan of boiling water 5 minutes. Rinse under cold running water 3 minutes. Drain. Place shank in heavy large saucepan with 2½ cups water and all remaining ingredients. Cover and cook over medium-high heat until tender, adding more water if necessary to maintain ½ inch of liquid in pan and turning twice, about 2¼ hours.

Transfer mixture to bowl, discarding star anise. Refrigerate at least 2 hours. (*Can be prepared 4 days ahead.*)

Cut beef across grain into ¹/₁₀-inch-thick slices. Overlap slices on platter. Let stand 20 minutes at room temperature before serving. (If gravy is desired, degrease cooking liquid, then warm and spoon over sliced beef.)

Madame Wu's Beef Sadea

Makes about 20 appetizers

1 pound flank steak, trimmed

Marinade
2 tablespoons dark soy sauce
1 teaspoon light soy sauce

1 teaspoon dry red wine
1 teaspoon Indian curry powder
1 teaspoon sugar

Trim about 1½ inches from one short end of meat and about 1 inch from the other end to square corners. Trim long ends to form rectangular shape. Wrap; freeze overnight.

Remove steak from freezer and let stand at room temperature until partially thawed, about 30 minutes. Cut steak across grain into about sixty ⅛-inch strips. Let thaw completely. Skewer 3 strips of beef ribbon-candy-fashion on 6-inch metal or wooden skewer. Repeat with remaining meat.

For marinade: Combine soy sauces, wine, curry powder and sugar in shallow dish and mix well. Roll beef in marinade to cover completely. Transfer to baking sheet. Cover and refrigerate 3 to 4 hours or overnight.

Lightly grease large skillet or griddle. Place over medium-high heat. Add skewers in batches and sauté on both sides until meat is browned, about 2 to 3 minutes. Serve immediately, or finish at the table over miniature hibachis.

Indonesian Herbed Beef Fritters with Coconut (Rempah)

Makes about 30

1 pound ground beef
1 cup grated fresh coconut
1 teaspoon ground coriander
2 garlic cloves, crushed
½ teaspoon ground cumin
½ teaspoon salt
½ teaspoon freshly ground pepper

¼ teaspoon Indonesian shrimp paste (trassi)
2 eggs, beaten to blend
2 teaspoons cornstarch
1 cup peanut oil
Colo Colo*

Combine beef, coconut, coriander, garlic, cumin, salt, pepper and shrimp paste in large bowl and blend well. Add eggs and cornstarch and mix thoroughly. Heat oil in wok or heavy large skillet over medium-high heat. Drop beef mixture into hot oil by heaping teaspoons (do not crowd) and fry until brown, turning occasionally, about 1 to 2 minutes. Remove fritters from oil using slotted spoon and drain on paper towels. Transfer to platter. Serve warm with colo colo.

*Colo Colo (Sweet and Sour Sauce)

This sauce should be pungent but not too hot. Salt and sugar can be adjusted according to personal preference.

Makes about ½ cup

2 shallots, sliced
2 tablespoons Kecap Manis (see page 13)
2 tablespoons peeled, seeded and chopped ripe tomato

2 tablespoons water
1 tablespoon fresh lime juice
1 teaspoon sliced fresh hot red chili
½ teaspoon sugar
½ teaspoon salt

Combine shallot, kecap manis, tomato, water, lime juice, chili, sugar and salt in processor or blender and mix until smooth. Turn into serving bowl. Cover and refrigerate. Bring to room temperature before serving.

Indonesian Spareribs (Babi Asam)

The butcher will saw the whole rib rack into three pieces. Served hot from the oven or at room temperature, these spicy ribs are great with cocktails or as part of an oriental menu.

6 appetizer servings

12 ounces dried tamarind pulp* with seeds
2 cups boiling water

6 small dried chilies, stemmed and seeded
¾ cup dried unsweetened coconut
¾ cup water
3 tablespoons sugar

3 tablespoons soy sauce
3 tablespoons fresh lime juice
6 large garlic cloves, crushed
¾ teaspoon ground coriander
2½ to 3 pounds pork spareribs, sawed crosswise into 3 strips and trimmed

Salt

Combine tamarind and 2 cups boiling water in small bowl, breaking up pulp with fork. Soak 1 hour.

Grind chilies in processor or blender. Add remaining ingredients except spareribs, salt and tamarind mixture. Pour tamarind through fine strainer into processor or blender, pressing through as much pulp as possible. Blend mixture 1 minute. Arrange spareribs in shallow glass dish. Pour marinade over, turning ribs to coat evenly. Refrigerate 6 to 8 hours, turning ribs occasionally.

Preheat oven to 325°F. Pat ribs dry (reserve marinade). Sprinkle ribs lightly with salt. Arrange on rack set over large shallow roasting pan containing 1 cup water. Roast 30 minutes. Turn ribs and brush with marinade. Continue cooking, brushing frequently with marinade and turning, until evenly browned, about 1 hour. Cut ribs apart. Serve hot.

Ribs can also be barbecued over medium-hot coals.

*A sour pulp surrounding seeds in fruit pods. Available at Indian and oriental markets and specialty food stores.

Saigon Crepe (Banh Xeo Saigon)

In Vietnam these crepes are usually prepared in a wok, but this recipe has been adapted for use with a skillet.

6 servings

Crepe Batter
1½ cups dried yellow mung beans

2 cups coconut milk
1 cup rice flour

12 tablespoons vegetable oil
12 thin slices pork loin or butt
6 uncooked shrimp, peeled, deveined and halved lengthwise

¾ cup bean sprouts
½ cup sliced mushrooms
1 small onion, thinly sliced into rings
Nuoc Cham (see page 21)
Vietnamese Vegetable Platter (see page 2)

For batter: Soak beans in enough water to cover for at least 2 hours or overnight. Drain well. Set aside ½ cup. Transfer remaining beans to small saucepan and cover with cold water. Place over high heat and bring to boil. Reduce heat to medium, cover and cook until water has evaporated, checking frequently, about 10 to 15 minutes. Remove from heat and set aside covered.

Mash the ½ cup uncooked beans in processor or blender. Add coconut milk and flour and blend well.

Heat 2 tablespoons oil in 8-inch nonstick or well seasoned skillet over medium-high heat. Add 2 slices of pork and 2 shrimp halves and fry until pork is cooked, about 1 minute. Add ½ cup batter and rotate skillet to spread mixture into thin pancake about 8 inches in diameter. Add 2 tablespoons bean sprouts, several mushroom slices, a few onion rings and 2 tablespoons reserved cooked mung beans. Cover skillet and cook pancake through, about 3 minutes. Fold pancake in half, transfer to heated platter and keep warm. Repeat, making 5 more crepes. Serve immediately, accompanied by nuoc cham sauce and the fresh vegetable platter.

Thai Pork and Crabmeat Rolls

Skewer and serve as an hors d'oeuvre.

10 buffet servings

1½ pounds ground pork
12 ounces cooked crabmeat, flaked
½ cup minced onion
½ cup roasted peanuts, skinned and coarsely chopped
⅓ cup cilantro leaves, chopped
¼ cup fish sauce (nam pla)
3 tablespoons coconut milk (or more)

3 medium garlic cloves, minced
½ teaspoon salt or to taste
⅓ teaspoon cayenne pepper or to taste
¼ teaspoon freshly ground pepper
Thai Sweet and Sour Vinegar and Garlic Sauce*

Preheat oven to 400°F. Mix all ingredients except sauce in large bowl, adding more coconut milk as necessary to moisten mixture for shaping. Form mixture into sausages using ¼ cup for each. Transfer to baking sheet. Bake until lightly browned and crisp, about 25 minutes, turning once. Skewer if desired. Serve rolls at room temperature with sauce for dipping.

*Thai Sweet and Sour Vinegar and Garlic Sauce

Makes about ¾ cup

⅓ cup white vinegar
¼ cup water
2 tablespoons sugar
2 tablespoons fish sauce (nam pla)

1 to 2 fresh red chilies, seeded and quartered
3 garlic cloves, halved

Puree all ingredients in blender until smooth. Serve at room temperature.

Vietnamese Spring Rolls with Dip (Cha Gio with Nuoc Cham)

The most popular dish in Vietnam, these rolls are usually filled with pork and crab, but any combination of meat, seafood or vegetables can be used. The Vietnamese version of Spring Rolls uses dried rice paper as a wrapper. The rolls can be prepared a day ahead, refrigerated and then fried without becoming soggy. Or they can be cooked ahead and kept warm for up to three hours. They can also be frozen and reheated.

Makes 60 Spring Rolls

Filling

2 tablespoons cloud ears (dried oriental mushrooms)

1 cup grated carrots
  Salt

1 pound boned and skinned chicken, cut into thin julienne (about 3 cups)

1 medium onion, finely chopped

2 garlic cloves, minced

2 shallots, minced

¼ teaspoon freshly ground pepper

15 dried rice paper wrappers (banh trang), each 12 inches in diameter

3 eggs, well beaten

  Vegetable oil
  Nuoc Cham*

For filling: Place cloud ears in small bowl. Cover with warm water and let stand 30 minutes to soften. Drain well; chop finely and transfer to large bowl.

Place carrots in colander. Sprinkle with salt and let stand several minutes to drain. Squeeze gently to remove excess liquid. Add to cloud ears and toss lightly. Add chicken, onion, garlic, shallots and pepper and mix well. Set aside.

Gently cut or fold each wrapper into fourths (they are very brittle and will break easily; any tears can be mended with beaten egg.) Paint wrappers thoroughly with egg and let stand several minutes to soften. Spoon 1 teaspoon filling in rectangular shape along curved edge of each wrapper. Roll wrapper once over filling, then fold in sides to enclose. Roll up completely.

Pour oil into skillet to depth of 1 inch. Arrange rolls in single layer in cold oil. Place over medium heat and fry about 10 minutes. Turn rolls and continue frying until golden. Remove from skillet using slotted spoon and drain on paper towels. Serve warm or at room temperature with Nuoc Cham for dipping.

---

*Nuoc Cham

No Vietnamese meal is served without this tangy sauce.

Makes about ¾ cup

1 tablespoon plus
  2 teaspoons sugar

4 garlic cloves

2 to 4 dried hot chili peppers or 2 fresh chili peppers

Juice and pulp of ¼ lime

5 tablespoons water

¼ cup fish sauce (nuoc mam)

Combine sugar, garlic and chilies in mortar and pound into paste (or mash with back of spoon in mixing bowl). Add lime juice and pulp and continue blending until well mixed. Add water and fish sauce and mix thoroughly. (*Sauce can be kept refrigerated about 1 week.*)

Philippine Crisp-fried Pork and Shrimp Dumplings (Lumpiang Sinkamas)

Makes about 4 dozen

12 ounces ³/₄-inch-thick pork loin chops
8 ounces peeled and deveined shrimp
2 green onions, cut into 1-inch lengths
1³/₄ pounds jícama, peeled and cut into ¹/₄-inch cubes
2 tablespoons oyster sauce

1 tablespoon soy sauce
1 tablespoon fresh lemon juice
1 tablespoon oriental sesame oil

All purpose flour
48 4-inch round won ton wrappers

48 green onion tops, blanched

Vegetable oil for deep frying

Broil pork chops until half cooked, about 4 minutes on each side. Cool to room temperature. Cut meat into 1-inch chunks and chop coarsely in processor. Add shrimp and 2 green onions and chop coarsely using on/off turns. Transfer to large bowl. Blend in jícama, oyster sauce, soy sauce, lemon juice and sesame oil. Cover and refrigerate while preparing wrappers. (*Filling can be prepared up to 1 day ahead.*)

Set pasta machine on thinnest setting. Flour won ton wrappers on both sides. Run through machine. Turn wrappers a half turn and run through machine a second time, forming 6-inch rounds (pull edges to form circle, if necessary).

Line baking sheet with waxed paper; dust lightly with flour. Pat green onion tops dry. Drain excess moisture in center of 1 wrapper. Gather wrapper around filling, forming pouch. Tie top of pouch close to filling with green onion top. Set on prepared sheet. Repeat with remaining filling and wrappers. (*Can be prepared up to 1 week ahead to this point and frozen. Wrap when frozen. Do not thaw before frying.*)

Heat oil in wok or deep heavy large skillet to 375°F. Add dumplings in batches (do not crowd) and fry until golden brown, about 8 minutes. Drain on paper towels. Serve immediately.

2 ❦ Soups

Traditional Asian menus, whether formal banquets or simple family lunches, always include a steaming bowl of soup. This selection showcases all manner of soups, from light broths to combinations of meat and vegetables that are substantial enough to make a meal in themselves.

In China, a large tureen is placed in the center of the table to be savored at leisure, much as a beverage would be. Ingredients vary from everyday vegetables to rare and expensive birds' nests, according to the occasion and to what the cook has on hand. At a banquet it is usual to enjoy a rich soup as a separate course, with a clear broth served elsewhere in the meal as a palate refresher.

This chapter illustrates the diversity of China's best recipes. The well-loved Mushroom Egg Drop Soup (page 29), featuring crisp bean sprouts and green onions, is the perfect first course for a party. For something more unusual, team Sesame Scones with Gingered Chinese Noodle Soup (page 27), a colorful mélange of vegetables and cellophane noodles; just add dessert and a fruity white wine or Chinese beer to make this a complete supper.

Soup is also extremely popular in Japan. The clear fish stock known as Dashi (page 4) is the basis for most soups, including Chicken and Shrimp Steamed in Custard (page 25), an intriguing dish that is often served as a palate refresher at a Japanese meal. The thicker soups served at breakfast or lunch often include fermented soybean paste, or miso. One such treat is Dote-Nabe (page 24), a savory blend of crisp vegetables and ocean-fresh oysters laced with a bit of saké.

Every bit as distinctive and delicious is Vietnamese Crabmeat Balls and Pearl Tapioca Soup (page 25), a combination of broth and crabmeat adapted from a traditional Vietnamese recipe. Along with spicy Fragrant Chicken Soup (page 27), popular in Malaysia, it is likely to become one of your favorite first courses—for Asian and occidental menus alike.

Spiced Singapore Cauliflower Soup

4 to 6 servings

8 cups beef stock
1 large onion, finely chopped
2 tablespoons Sherry
1 tablespoon ground coriander
1 large garlic clove, minced
1 teaspoon ground cumin

¼ teaspoon freshly ground pepper
¼ teaspoon ground mace
1 medium head cauliflower, cored and coarsely chopped
1 7¾-ounce package bean thread noodles

Combine first 8 ingredients in 4-quart saucepan and bring to boil over medium-high heat. Reduce heat and simmer 10 minutes. Add cauliflower and return to boil. Cook 4 minutes. Break up noodles in medium bowl and soak in hot water 30 seconds to separate strands. Drain thoroughly and add to soup. Return to boil and continue cooking until noodles are tender, about 2 minutes. Ladle into bowls and serve hot.

Dote-Nabe

This hearty Japanese soup is a great party dish.

4 servings

1 cup Fish Stock*
2 cups water
½ cup miso
2 tablespoons saké or dry white wine
2 small carrots, peeled and cut into ½-inch rounds
12 enoki mushrooms or 6 sliced button mushrooms
4 large dried shiitake mushrooms, soaked 30 minutes, hard stems discarded

8 ounces Chinese cabbage, cut into wedges
1 medium onion, halved and thinly sliced
1 pound shucked fresh oysters
2 tofu cakes, cut into large squares
4 green onions, cut into ¼-inch pieces
4 chrysanthemum leaves, trimmed (optional)
1 cup water

Heat stock in heavy Dutch oven or large saucepan. Add 2 cups water. Stir in miso a little at a time, pressing against sides of pan with spoon to dissolve. Stir in wine. Add remaining ingredients except water in order listed. Simmer 3 minutes. Add 1 cup water and simmer 2 minutes. Ladle soup into bowls and serve.

*Fish Stock

Makes about 2 quarts

2 tablespoons (¼ stick) butter
2 pounds fish bones, washed
3 quarts water
2 large onions, coarsely chopped
2 large carrots, coarsely chopped
1 large celery stalk with leaves, cut into large chunks
4 garlic cloves, halved

1 small piece peeled fresh ginger (optional)
6 to 8 black peppercorns
2 large bay leaves
½ teaspoon *each* dried thyme, tarragon, summer savory and oregano, crumbled

Melt butter in stockpot over medium-high heat. Stir in fish bones to coat with butter. Add remaining ingredients and bring to boil. Reduce heat and simmer 30 minutes. Strain. Store stock in airtight container.

Japanese Oyster-Chive Soup

4 servings

3 cups water
1 5- to 6-inch piece dashi-konbu (dried kelp)
8 ounces shucked fresh oysters with liquor

2 tofu cakes, cut into 1-inch pieces
3½ tablespoons miso
4 oriental long chives, snipped
Pinch of dried red pepper flakes

Heat 3 cups water and kelp in 2-quart saucepan. Discard kelp just before water begins to boil. As soon as water comes to boil, add oysters and tofu. Return to boiling, skimming foam from surface. Mix miso with 1 teaspoon hot soup. Stir mixture back into pan. Add chives and pepper flakes and return to boil. Remove from heat. Ladle into bowls and serve.

Vietnamese Crabmeat Balls and Pearl Tapioca Soup (Sup Cua Bot Bang)

Tapioca gives this the slightly gelatinous texture often found in oriental soups.

8 to 10 servings

4 ounces ground pork
2 shallots, finely chopped
1 egg yolk
1 teaspoon tomato paste
1 teaspoon fish sauce (nuoc mam)
Freshly ground pepper
8 ounces fresh or thawed frozen crabmeat

6 cups chicken stock, preferably homemade
½ cup small pearl tapioca
2 tablespoons fish sauce
2 tablespoons chopped cilantro
2 tablespoons chopped green onion (green part only)

Combine pork, shallots, egg yolk, tomato paste, 1 teaspoon fish sauce and pepper in medium bowl and blend until smooth. Add crabmeat and mix gently but thoroughly (crab should retain texture). Shape into ¾-inch balls.

Bring stock to boil in large saucepan. Add crabmeat balls and boil until cooked through, about 10 to 15 minutes. Meanwhile, soak tapioca 5 minutes in enough water to cover. Drain well. Stir into soup and boil another 2 minutes. Blend in 2 tablespoons fish sauce. Ladle into tureen or individual bowls and sprinkle with pepper. Garnish with cilantro and green onion.

Soup can be cooked ahead and reheated.

Chicken and Shrimp Steamed in Custard (Chawan Mushi)

This is often served as a palate refresher toward the end of a Japanese meal.

4 servings

4 medium-size uncooked shrimp, shelled, deveined and halved lengthwise
½ chicken breast, skinned, boned and cut into ½-inch cubes
4 dried mushrooms (preferably shiitake), softened 30 minutes in warm water to cover, drained and squeezed dry
3 canned ginkgo nuts, drained

2 cups dashi (basic stock; see page 4) or light chicken or fish stock
4 eggs, beaten to blend
2 tablespoons mirin (syrupy rice wine) or dry Sherry
½ teaspoon Japanese soy sauce
4 young spinach leaves
4 lemon wedges

Lightly oil four 8-ounce ovenproof dishes or custard cups. Divide shrimp, chicken, dried mushrooms and ginkgo nuts evenly among dishes.

Combine dashi, eggs, mirin and soy sauce in bowl and mix well. Divide egg mixture evenly among dishes. Float 1 spinach leaf on each. Cover each dish tightly with lightly oiled aluminum foil. Set dishes in steamer. Add water to steamer to depth of 1½ inches and bring to boil over medium heat. Cover partially and steam until custard is firm, about 10 to 12 minutes. Remove from heat and discard foil. Serve custard hot. Garnish with lemon.

Chinese Chicken-Corn Soup

4 servings

1½ cups chicken stock
1 whole chicken breast, skinned, boned and cubed (about 4½ ounces)
1 16½-ounce can cream-style corn
1 15-ounce can straw mushrooms, drained

4 to 4½ ounces tofu, mashed
2 tablespoons Sherry
1 tablespoon cornstarch
2 eggs, beaten to blend

Bring stock to rolling boil in large saucepan. Stir in chicken, corn, mushrooms and tofu and return to boil, stirring frequently. Reduce heat to medium and simmer 2 to 3 minutes. Meanwhile, combine Sherry and cornstarch in small bowl. Stir Sherry mixture and eggs into soup. Continue cooking until soup is thickened, about 1 minute. Serve immediately, or cool slightly, chill and reheat.

Jewel Jellied Chicken Soup

6 servings

8 cups water
3 ⅛-inch-thick slices peeled ginger
3 green onions
1 teaspoon salt
1 2½- to 3-pound chicken

2 tablespoons dry Sherry
15 whole peppercorns

2 whole star anise
3 ounces Virginia or Black Forest ham, cut into matchsticks

Shredded romaine
Cilantro sprigs

Combine water, ginger, onions and salt in 8-quart saucepan and bring to boil. Add chicken, cover and return to gentle boil. Reduce heat and simmer 30 minutes. Remove chicken and cool slightly; reserve stock.

Remove meat from chicken and cut into cubes or strips; set aside. Return skin, bones and carcass to stock. Add Sherry, peppercorns and star anise. Bring to boil. Reduce heat, cover and simmer 3 hours. Strain stock; discard solids. Stir ham and chicken into stock. (*Can be prepared 2 days ahead.*)

Cover and refrigerate soup until chilled and slightly jellied. Just before serving, degrease soup if necessary. Place several shreds of romaine in bottom of each bowl. Add soup. Top each with cilantro sprig.

Fragrant Chicken Soup (Soto Ayam)

The Paddock restaurant in the Kuala Lumpur Hilton specializes in Malay luncheons daily. This is one of the most-requested dishes.

4 to 6 servings

1 3-pound chicken, cut into serving pieces
2 quarts cold water
1 medium onion, chopped
1 fresh lemongrass stalk, finely chopped and pounded, or 1 strip lemon peel
12 black peppercorns
2 teaspoons salt or to taste

1 medium onion, chopped
6 shallots, minced
¼ cup grated fresh ginger
2 garlic cloves, minced
2 tablespoons vegetable oil

3 tablespoons cold water
1 tablespoon ground poppy seeds

1 teaspoon ground coriander
½ teaspoon freshly ground white pepper
½ teaspoon ground aniseed
½ teaspoon ground cumin

1 fresh lemongrass stalk or 1 strip lemon peel
3 3-inch cinnamon sticks
3 sections star anise

Vegetable oil for deep frying
½ cup sliced shallots

½ cup finely chopped green onion
¼ cup cilantro leaves

Bone chicken breasts, reserving bones. Cut breast meat into ¼-inch-thick strips. Wrap tightly and refrigerate. Combine breast bones and remaining chicken in large saucepan with 2 quarts water. Bring to boil, skimming surface occasionally. Add 1 onion, 1 chopped lemongrass stalk, peppercorns and salt. Simmer 1 hour. Strain stock; reserve cooked chicken meat for another use. Discard vegetables.

Puree 1 onion, 6 shallots, ginger and garlic in processor or blender. Heat 2 tablespoons oil in another heavy large saucepan over low heat. Add onion mixture and stir 5 minutes.

Mix 3 tablespoons water, poppy seeds, coriander, white pepper, aniseed and cumin to taste. Blend into onion mixture. Stir for 3 minutes.

Bring stock to simmer in medium saucepan. Stir in onion mixture, 1 lemongrass stalk, cinnamon and star anise. Simmer 20 minutes.

Meanwhile, heat oil in deep fryer or small saucepan to 375°F. Add ½ cup shallots and fry until golden, about 1 minute. Drain on paper towels.

Add chicken breast strips to soup and simmer until just opaque, about 3 minutes. Discard lemongrass, cinnamon and star anise. Garnish soup with fried shallots, green onion and cilantro.

Gingered Chinese Noodle Soup

Thin spaghetti can be substituted for the cellophane noodles. Use one generous cup spaghetti broken into three-inch pieces; cook in boiling water until al dente, then drain.

4 to 6 servings

3 ounces cellophane noodles

2 tablespoons vegetable oil
1 medium onion, sliced
2 thin carrots, sliced diagonally
2 medium garlic cloves, minced
1 teaspoon minced fresh ginger
1 medium-size red bell pepper, thinly sliced
3 cups chicken stock
1½ cups water
1 tablespoon soy sauce
1 cup Smithfield or Black Forest ham, cut into julienne (about 4 ounces)

1 cup shredded watercress leaves
½ cup thinly sliced mushrooms
1 cup (generous) snow peas, strings removed
1 teaspon oriental sesame oil or to taste
1 teaspoon rice vinegar or to taste Pinch of dried red pepper flakes
2 green onions, thinly sliced on diagonal Sesame Scones*

Place cellophane noodles in large bowl. Cover with boiling water. Let stand 5 minutes. Drain thoroughly.

Heat oil in wok or deep large skillet over medium-high heat. Add onion and carrots and stir-fry 3 minutes. Add garlic and ginger, then bell pepper. Stir-fry 30 seconds. Add stock, water and soy sauce. Cover and boil 2 minutes. Add ham, watercress, mushrooms and noodles. Return to boil. Cover, turn off heat and let steep 2 minutes. Add snow peas, cover and let steep until vegetables are crisp-tender, about 3 minutes. Stir in sesame oil, rice vinegar and red pepper flakes. Adjust seasoning. Ladle soup into deep bowls. Sprinkle with green onions. Accompany with sesame scones.

*Sesame Scones

A new variation on an old favorite. Serve with lots of butter.

Makes 10

2 cups unbleached all purpose flour	1 tablespoon honey
2 teaspoons baking powder	1 teaspoon oriental sesame oil
1 teaspoon baking soda	⅓ cup (or more) buttermilk
½ teaspoon salt	
½ cup (1 stick) chilled unsalted butter, cut into pieces	1 egg, beaten to blend (glaze) Sesame seeds
2 eggs	

Preheat oven to 425°F. Butter baking sheet. Sift flour, baking powder, baking soda and salt into medium bowl. Cut in ½ cup butter until coarse meal forms. Make well in center of dry ingredients. Add 2 eggs, honey, sesame oil and ⅓ cup buttermilk to well; blend with fork. Stir into dry ingredients, adding enough buttermilk to form sticky but workable dough.

Gently pat dough into 1-inch-thick round on floured surface. Cut dough into 10 wedges, cutting straight down with sharp, floured knife. Brush each wedge lightly with glaze. Place sesame seeds on plate. Dip glazed top of each wedge into seeds. Arrange sesame side up on prepared sheet, spacing ½ inch apart. Bake until golden brown, 12 to 15 minutes. Serve hot.

Chrysanthemum Soup

4 to 6 servings

2 large dried Japanese mushrooms	1 teaspoon light soy sauce or to taste
3 cups homemade chicken stock or 2 13½-ounce cans chicken stock, warmed	Petals of 1 large chrysanthemum, well washed and drained (garnish)
¼ cup Sherry	

Soak mushrooms in warm broth several hours. Strain, reserving broth. Cut mushrooms into small strips, discarding hard stems. Combine reserved broth with all remaining ingredients except chrysanthemum petals in medium saucepan and simmer about 10 minutes. Stir in chrysanthemum petals, ladle into individual bowls and serve immediately.

Chinese Hot Pot Soup

Use the microwave to
create this quick dish.

4 to 6 servings

½ pound lean ground beef
2 14½-ounce cans beef stock
2¾ cups water
1 10-ounce package frozen Chinese
   stir-fry vegetables

½ cup instant rice
¼ cup sliced green onion
1 tablespoon soy sauce

Crumble beef into 1½-quart ovenproof glass baking dish. Cook on High 1½ minutes. Crumble with fork and cook on High until browned, about 1½ minutes. Pour off fat. Add remaining ingredients. Cover and cook on High 10 minutes, stirring once or twice. Serve hot.

Celery Egg Drop Soup

10 servings

½ cup parsley leaves,
   thoroughly dried

2 large celery stalks, strings
   removed, cut into 1-inch pieces
5 cups chicken stock
1 teaspoon dark soy sauce

½ teaspoon oriental sesame oil
   Salt
   Dash of cayenne pepper

1 large egg
1 teaspoon vegetable oil

In food processor fitted with steel knife, mince parsley using on/off turns. Remove and set aside for garnish.

Stack celery horizontally in feed tube and, using medium shredder, shred using light pressure. Transfer to 2-quart saucepan and add stock, soy sauce and sesame oil. Simmer uncovered 10 minutes. Taste and adjust seasoning with salt and cayenne pepper.

Using plastic or steel knife, combine egg and oil and process briefly to blend.

Remove soup from heat and drizzle in beaten egg. When egg is set, stir gently to distribute evenly. Ladle into bowls, garnish with parsley and serve.

Chinese-style Mushroom Egg Drop Soup

8 to 10 servings

1½ quarts chicken stock or
   vegetable stock
6 ounces mushrooms, sliced
3 ounces fresh spinach, coarsely
   shredded or chopped
1 to 2 quarter-size slices fresh
   ginger, peeled and minced
1 to 2 garlic cloves, minced
2 tablespoons plus 2 teaspoons
   soy sauce
½ teaspoon sugar
⅛ teaspoon freshly ground pepper
⅛ teaspoon crushed red
   pepper flakes

¼ cup dry Sherry
2 tablespoons cornstarch

2 ounces vermicelli, cooked and
   drained

1 egg, beaten to blend
1 tablespoon oriental sesame oil
8 ounces fresh bean sprouts
½ bunch green onions, chopped

Bring stock to boil in large pot over high heat. Reduce heat, add next 8 ingredients and simmer about 30 minutes.

Mix Sherry and cornstarch in measuring cup to form a thin paste. Set aside.

Ten minutes before serving, bring soup to boil. Stir cornstarch mixture to remove any lumps. Blend into soup in slow steady stream. Cook soup, stirring constantly, until clear and slightly thickened. Stir in vermicelli. Remove from heat.

Pour in egg slowly, then stir gently with fork until egg forms light strands. Stir in sesame oil. Divide bean sprouts and green onion among soup bowls and ladle hot soup over. Serve immediately.

Meatball Rice Noodle Soup

A food processor makes quick work of chopping the ingredients for this fragrant dish.

6 servings

2 large shallots (2 ounces total)
1 large garlic clove
1 ⅛ × ¾-inch piece fresh ginger, peeled
1 slice soft white bread, crust trimmed, quartered
¼ cup milk
2 tablespoons plus 1 teaspoon fish sauce* (nuoc mam)
½ teaspoon salt
⅛ teaspoon cinnamon
⅛ teaspoon freshly ground pepper
12 ounces lean beef, cut into 1-inch cubes

2 medium onions (8 ounces total), halved

3 quarter-size slices peeled fresh ginger
1¾ cups rich beef stock (preferably homemade)
1¾ cups rich chicken stock (preferably homemade)
2½ cups water
2 ounces rice vermicelli, broken into thirds

4 large green onions (3 ounces total), including green tops, cut into feed-tube lengths
6 leaves green leaf lettuce (3 ounces total)
¼ cup fresh cilantro leaves

With food processor machine running, drop shallots, garlic and 1 piece ginger through feed tube and mince. Add bread and process to fine crumbs. Mix in milk, 1 teaspoon fish sauce, salt, cinnamon and pepper using on/off turns, stopping to scrape down sides of work bowl. Add beef and process until ground using on/off turns. Shape mixture into 1-inch rounds.

Slice onions in processor using firm pressure. Transfer to 4-quart saucepan. Add ginger slices, both stocks, water and remaining 2 tablespoons fish sauce. Cover and bring to simmer over medium-high heat. Add meatballs and vermicelli. Reduce heat and simmer gently until meat is cooked through, about 5 minutes. Remove soup from heat. Discard ginger. (*Can be prepared 3 days ahead, covered and refrigerated. Bring to simmer before continuing.*)

Using thick slicer, stand green onions in feed tube and slice using light pressure. Arrange lettuce in feed tube and slice using light pressure. Mix green onions, lettuce and cilantro into soup. Adjust seasoning. Serve immediately.

3 ❧ Rice and Noodles

Rice and noodles are so central to oriental cooking that no meal is considered complete without one or the other. Indeed, even the most copious Chinese banquet typically concludes with a bowl of plain steamed rice, just in case the diners are not yet satisfied. Whether served as an accompaniment, in a combination dish or as a snack, rice and noodles find their way into a multitude of recipes.

In ancient times, wealth was often measured in terms of the amount of rice one possessed, and throughout the centuries numerous works of Asian poetry and art have been dedicated to this pearl-like grain. While Western cooks are more familiar with long-grain rice, oriental dishes often work best with the short-grain variety: It is sticky enough to form clumps, making it easier to eat with chopsticks. Perfect Boiled Rice—Oriental Method (page 32) or Japanese Steamed Rice (page 32) can be used in recipes calling for cooked rice or served alone as a side dish. Long-grain rice does appear in some combination dishes, however, such as Hué Rice (page 33). This sophisticated Vietnamese specialty is as attractive as it is flavorful, with a pinwheel of savory garnishes embellishing tender rice.

Noodles are believed by many to have originated in Asia, and they are indisputably as tasty and versatile in oriental cooking as in Italian. Wheat-based *udon*, cooked al dente, is blended with shiitake mushrooms and a light coat of tangy dressing for a lovely Japanese Noodle Salad (page 41). *Mai fun* (rice stick noodles) puff up dramatically when dropped into hot oil, forming a "nest" for Western-style Stir-fry (page 43) filled with plump pieces of chicken, shrimp and vegetables.

 Rice

Perfect Boiled Rice—Oriental Method

6 servings

1 cup medium- or short-grain white rice
3/4 teaspoon salt

1/8 teaspoon freshly ground white pepper

Combine rice, salt and pepper in heavy 2- to 3-quart saucepan. Add enough water to cover rice by 1 inch. Bring to boil over high heat. Reduce heat, cover and simmer until water is absorbed, about 20 minutes. Remove from heat and let stand, covered, 5 to 10 minutes before serving.

Japanese Steamed Rice (Gohan)

Rice is the backbone of Japanese cuisine and no meal is considered complete without it. Even the most sumptuous dinner ends with a bowl of steamed rice so the host will be sure that the guests have had enough to eat.

Makes 6 cups cooked rice

2 cups Japanese or other short-or medium-grain rice

2 1/2 cups cold water
1 teaspoon salt (optional)

Pour rice into strainer and rinse with cold water until water runs clear. Drain well. Transfer rice to heavy deep saucepan with tight-fitting lid. Add 2 1/2 cups cold water and salt if desired. Let stand 30 minutes to 1 hour.

Place saucepan over high heat and bring to boil. Cover, reduce heat to lowest setting and cook 15 minutes; *do not remove lid during cooking.* Turn off heat and let rice stand, covered, 10 minutes.

Japanese Vinegared Rice

4 to 6 servings

1/4 cup rice vinegar
1 tablespoon sugar
2 cups freshly cooked rice, cooled
Crumbled nori (dried seaweed or laver), optional

Lettuce leaves

Combine vinegar and sugar in large bowl. Blend in rice and seaweed.

To serve, pack mixture into ice cream scoop (or small cup or bowl) and unmold onto lettuce leaves.

Japanese Fluffy Rice with Vegetables and Seaweed (Maze Gohan)

8 servings

3 3/4 cups water
2 cups rice
1/4 cup saké or dry Sherry
2 tablespoons Japanese soy sauce
2 teaspoons shichimi tōgarashi (dried blend of hot spices)
2 cups diced cooked carrot (3 to 4 large)

1 sheet (about 4 × 8 inches) nori (dried seaweed or laver), optional garnish
1 cup cooked peas

Combine water, rice, saké, soy sauce and spices in large saucepan and bring to boil over high heat. Reduce heat to low, cover tightly and cook until all liquid is absorbed, about 25 minutes. Add carrot and toss lightly. Cover and place over very low heat until carrot is heated through, stirring gently once or twice. Remove from heat.

Toast seaweed lightly in dry skillet over high heat until crisp. Set aside. Add peas to rice and blend well. Place over high heat and warm briefly. Turn into large serving bowl. Crumble seaweed over top and serve immediately.

Hué Rice (Com Am Phu)

In this Vietnamese specialty each diner receives a mound of rice completely covered with a pinwheel of different garnishes. Tangy nuoc cham *sauce is used as a condiment.*

8 servings

Egg Pancake
8 eggs, separated
1 teaspoon fish sauce (nuoc mam)
1 teaspoon water
   Freshly ground pepper
4 teaspoons vegetable oil

Pork
3 garlic cloves
3 shallots
1 tablespoon fish sauce
2 teaspoons sugar
¼ teaspoon freshly ground pepper
12 ounces lean pork, thinly sliced

Cucumber
1 large cucumber
½ teaspoon salt

Cotton Shrimp
8 ounces uncooked shrimp
½ teaspoon fish sauce
   Freshly ground pepper
1½ teaspoons vegetable oil
1 shallot, chopped
1 garlic clove, chopped

Rice
3¼ cups water
2 cups long-grain rice

   Cilantro sprigs
   Nuoc Cham (see page 21)

For pancake: Beat egg whites in large bowl with ½ teaspoon fish sauce, ½ teaspoon water and a pinch of pepper. Beat yolks in separate bowl with remaining fish sauce, water and pepper. Heat 2 teaspoons oil in large skillet over medium heat. Add egg whites, rotating skillet to spread mixture into thin pancake. Cook until firm; turn and cook other side. Transfer to plate and let cool. Repeat with remaining oil and yolk mixture, cooking in same manner. When cooled, roll up each pancake and cut into thin strips. Set aside.

For pork: Combine garlic, shallots, fish sauce, sugar and pepper in mortar and pound to paste (or mash with back of spoon in mixing bowl). Spread evenly over pork and let stand 30 minutes.

Preheat broiler. Broil pork until done, turning once, about 5 to 8 minutes per side. Cut into thin strips and let cool.

For cucumber: Peel cucumber and cut in half lengthwise. Cut crosswise into thin slices. Transfer to colander, sprinkle with salt and let stand 5 minutes. Rinse well; drain and squeeze gently.

For shrimp: Peel and devein shrimp. Rinse under cold water and pat dry with paper towels. Cut into thin crosswise slices. Sprinkle with fish sauce and pepper. Heat oil in small skillet over medium-high heat. Add shallot and garlic and sauté until browned. Add shrimp and cook, stirring constantly, until opaque. Transfer to mortar and pound to smooth paste (or mash with back of spoon in mixing bowl). Return shrimp to dry skillet and cook over medium heat, mashing with back of spoon until all moisture is removed and shrimp is browned. Remove from heat and set aside (can be stored in tightly covered jar in refrigerator for several weeks).

For rice: Combine water and rice in saucepan and bring to boil over high heat. Let boil 3 to 4 minutes. Cover, reduce heat to low and continue cooking 20 minutes. Remove from heat and let stand, covered, 20 minutes.

To assemble: Mound rice in center of each plate. Arrange pork, cucumber, shrimp and strips of egg-white pancake separately in pinwheel pattern over top so no rice shows. Surround with strips of yolk pancake. Garnish with cilantro. Serve immediately with nuoc cham.

Wild Rice with Shiitake Mushrooms

The earthy taste of the mushrooms is delicious with wild rice.

6 servings

3 cups water
1 cup wild rice
½ teaspoon salt
5 tablespoons butter

8 ounces fresh shiitake mushrooms, stems trimmed
Salt and freshly ground pepper

Bring water, rice and ½ teaspoon salt to boil in heavy medium saucepan. Reduce heat to low, cover and cook 45 minutes. Drain well. Transfer rice to medium baking dish. Mix in 2 tablespoons butter. Set aside.

Preheat oven to 250°F. Melt remaining 3 tablespoons butter in heavy large skillet over high heat. Add mushrooms and stir until tender, about 4 minutes. Mix into rice. Season with salt and pepper. Cover and bake 20 minutes to blend flavors. Serve hot.

Green Fried Rice with Shrimp

8 servings

1 cup parsley leaves, thoroughly dried
4 large shallots
2 cups water
1 cup long-grain converted rice
2 tablespoons (¼ stick) butter
1½ teaspoons salt

2 large garlic cloves, peeled
2 medium green peppers, seeded and cut into chunks

3 tablespoons vegetable oil

1 pound frozen shrimp, shelled and deveined, *unthawed*
8 large mushrooms, washed and patted dry

1 tablespoon soy sauce
16 snow peas (preferably fresh), trimmed
1 10-ounce package frozen tiny peas, thawed
Dash of cayenne pepper
Salt

In food processor, mince parsley using on/off turns. Remove and set aside. Mince shallots by dropping through feed tube with machine running. Combine shallots, water, rice, butter and salt in medium saucepan. Place over medium-high heat, bring to boil, stir through once, then cover and simmer 15 to 20 minutes, or until all liquid is absorbed. Remove from heat and let stand, covered, for an additional 10 minutes. Fluff with fork, let cool briefly and then chill at least 2 hours, preferably overnight.

Mince garlic by dropping through feed tube of food processor with machine running; remove and set aside. Add green peppers and chop coarsely using on/off turns; remove.

Heat 1 tablespoon oil in wok or large skillet over medium heat. Add garlic and sauté until lightly browned.

Rinse frozen shrimp under cold water, allowing to defrost slightly but still remain firm (a knife should be able to penetrate shrimp). Using medium slicer, slice shrimp, using firm pressure; remove and set aside. Slice mushrooms, using light pressure.

Add shrimp to garlic in wok and cook over medium-high heat until shrimp just turns opaque; *do not overcook.* remove and set aside. Add remaining oil to wok and heat thoroughly. Add mushrooms and stir-fry 2 minutes. Add rice and soy sauce and stir-fry 3 minutes over high heat. Add green peppers, snow peas and peas and heat through. Mix in shrimp, parsley, cayenne and salt to taste and cook only until heated through. Taste and adjust seasoning. Serve immediately.

Asparagus Fried Rice

Feel free to substitute other vegetables for the asparagus, depending on what is available in the market and what you prefer. Vegetables should be crisp-tender for contrasting textures.

8 servings

2 cups water
1 cup long-grain converted rice
2 tablespoons (¼ stick) unsalted butter
2 large shallots (1 ounce total), minced
1½ teaspoons salt

2 pounds fresh asparagus spears, stems peeled

1 cup parsley leaves, minced
8 medium green onions (4 ounces total), cut into thirds and sliced in food processor
Salt and freshly ground white pepper

2½ tablespoons peanut oil

Combine first 5 ingredients in small saucepan and bring to boil. Stir through once, reduce heat to low, cover and simmer until liquid is absorbed, about 15 minutes. Remove from heat and let stand, covered, 10 minutes. Fluff rice with fork, let cool and refrigerate.

Cut 1½ inches from tips of asparagus spears and set aside. Insert medium slicer into food processor and wedge stems vertically in feed tube. Slice, using medium pressure. Blanch stems 30 seconds in 1 quart rapidly boiling water mixed with 2 teaspoons salt. Remove with strainer or slotted spoon, maintaining water at boil. Run stems under cold water until cold to touch; drain well and set aside. Blanch asparagus tips 30 seconds in same water; cool and drain well.

Add sliced asparagus stems, parsley, onion, salt and pepper to rice.

At serving time, heat 2 tablespoons oil in large skillet over medium-high heat until sizzling. Add rice and quickly heat through, stirring gently.

Heat remaining oil in small skillet over medium-high heat. Add asparagus tips and quickly heat through. Sprinkle over rice and serve immediately.

 Noodles

Oriental Noodles

6 servings

1 12-ounce package Japanese-style water noodles (udon)
¼ cup vegetable oil

18 large green onions including green tops (18 ounces total), trimmed and cut into processor feed tube lengths

1 6-ounce can whole water chestnuts, drained, opposite ends cut flat
¼ cup toasted sesame seeds
1 teaspoon ground coriander
½ teaspoon salt
¼ cup chicken stock

Bring 2 quarts water to boil in 6-quart saucepan over medium-high heat. Meanwhile, rinse noodles under cold running water until all of potato starch coating is removed. Add noodles to boiling water and bring to boil, stirring frequently to separate. Pour in ½ cup cold water. Return to boil, stirring frequently. Repeat 3 times, adding ½ cup cold water each time. Continue cooking, stirring frequently, until noodles are tender, about 5 minutes. Drain and rinse noodles under cold running water. Drain again. Combine noodles and ¼ cup oil in saucepan and toss well.

Place green onions vertically in processor feed tube and slice using light pressure with medium slicer. Stack water chestnuts in feed tube flat side down and slice using medium pressure. Add onion and water chestnuts to noodles. Add sesame seeds, coriander and salt and toss well. Add stock and cook, stirring gently, over medium heat until warmed through. Serve immediately.

Cold Noodles in Sesame Sauce

Serve this as an appetizer, or for a light lunch or supper with a tossed salad.

4 servings

8 ounces vermicelli or Chinese noodles
1 tablespoon oriental sesame oil

3 tablespoons peanut butter
3 tablespoons water
2 tablespoons soy sauce
2 tablespoons sesame seed paste (tahini)
1 tablespoon peanut oil
1 tablespoon Sherry

2 teaspoons vinegar
1½ teaspoons sugar
2 garlic cloves, mashed to a paste
1 ½-inch piece ginger, mashed to a paste
¼ to ½ teaspoon Chinese chili oil *or* red pepper flakes
Freshly ground pepper

Chopped green onion and shredded cucumber (garnish)

Cook pasta according to package directions. Drain well. Transfer to mixing bowl and add sesame oil, tossing lightly to coat. Cover and chill at least 2 hours.

Combine all remaining ingredients except garnish and blend well. Mound noodles on platter and spoon sauce over top. Sprinkle with green onion and cucumber. (*Sauce can be made ahead. Bring to room temperature before serving.*)

Cellophane Noodle and Seafood Salad

Delicate cellophane noodles are delicious in cold dishes, as in this distinctively sesame-flavored salad.

5 to 6 servings

Dressing
½ cup fresh lemon juice
⅓ cup minced green onion
¼ cup peanut oil
2 tablespoons oriental sesame oil
1 tablespoon soy sauce
¾ teaspoon salt
½ teaspoon Chinese red chili oil *or* hot pepper sauce to taste
½ teaspoon sugar

Salad
1 7¾-ounce package cellophane noodles (long rice or saifun)

1 pound unshelled small raw shrimp
1 pound scallops
2 cups thinly sliced celery (peeled, if desired)
1 or 2 large cucumbers, peeled, halved lengthwise, seeded and sliced thinly into crescents (garnish)

Combine all ingredients for dressing in jar with tight-fitting lid and shake well.

Soak noodles in hot water to cover 30 minutes. Drop into boiling salted water, return to boil and cook 1 minute. Immediately drain into colander and run under cold water until cooled completely. Transfer to large bowl. Add half of dressing and toss lightly.

Combine shrimp and scallops in covered steamer and cook until barely tender, about 2 to 3 minutes (or simmer gently in just enough water to cover). Drain into colander. Peel and devein shrimp and cut scallops horizontally into 1/2-inch slices. Add to noodles with celery and remaining dressing and toss lightly. Cover and chill at least 2 hours. To serve, mound salad in center of platter and surround with cucumber.

Chicken and Japanese Buckwheat Noodles in Peanut Sauce

6 servings

3 pounds chicken thighs and legs (about 4 cups cooked chicken)
1 carrot, cut into chunks
1 stalk celery, sliced

1/2 cup water
1/3 cup soy sauce
2 tablespoons dark brown sugar
1 tablespoon freshly grated ginger
1 1/2 teaspoons ground coriander
1 teaspoon grated lemon zest

2 tablespoons peanut oil
1/3 cup sliced green onion
2 to 3 tiny dried hot peppers, seeded and chopped *or*
1/4 teaspoon hot pepper flakes

1 1/2 teaspoons minced garlic
1/3 cup roasted unsalted peanuts
1/4 cup fresh lemon juice

7 ounces buckwheat noodles (soba) *or* linguine

2 tablespoons rice wine vinegar
1 teaspoon sugar
1/8 teaspoon salt
4 cups torn fresh spinach leaves
1 small hot red pepper (optional)

Combine chicken, carrot and celery in large saucepan or Dutch oven with enough lightly salted water to cover. Bring to boil, then reduce heat and simmer gently 20 to 25 minutes. Remove from heat and cool chicken in broth. Discard skin and bone and tear chicken into fine slivers. Transfer to bowl, cover and chill.

Combine next 6 ingredients in small saucepan and blend well. Place over medium-high heat and bring to boil. Remove from heat and set aside.

Heat oil in small skillet over medium-high heat. Add onion, peppers and garlic and sauté until lightly colored. Transfer to food processor or blender and add peanuts and soy sauce mixture. Blend until very smooth. Press through fine sieve into small saucepan. Bring to boil, stirring constantly, then reduce heat and simmer 2 minutes. Cool slightly and stir in lemon juice.

Cook noodles in boiling water until just tender. Drain well and transfer to mixing bowl. Add half of peanut sauce and toss lightly. Add remaining sauce to chicken and blend well. (*Salad may be prepared 1 day ahead to this point.*)

To serve, combine vinegar, sugar and salt in mixing bowl and blend well. Add spinach and toss thoroughly. Arrange around edge of large deep platter. Pile noodles in center and top with chicken. Slice pepper into flowerlike shape and remove seeds. Place on chicken.

Red Pepper Noodle Salad with Hot and Sour Dressing

These noodles are the color of a memorable sunset, but—if you must— any fresh pasta can be substituted.

6 servings

3 red bell peppers

2 cups all purpose flour
1 egg
1 tablespoon oriental sesame oil
1 teaspoon salt

2 tablespoons oriental sesame oil
2 tablespoons vegetable oil
3 medium zucchini, halved lengthwise and sliced into half-rounds
6 green onions, cut on diagonal into ½-inch pieces, including some green tops
2 tablespoons toasted sesame seeds

Dressing
1 cup plus 2 tablespoons rice vinegar
¾ cup chicken stock
6 tablespoons creamy peanut butter
6 tablespoons soy sauce
4 garlic cloves, minced
3 tablespoons oriental sesame oil
3 tablespoons minced fresh ginger
3 teaspoons chili oil
3 teaspoons dried red pepper flakes

Char peppers over gas flame or in broiler until blackened on all sides. Wrap in paper bag and let stand 10 minutes to steam. Peel and seed. Rinse if necessary; pat dry. Puree in blender. Transfer to heavy small saucepan and cook over medium heat until all liquid has evaporated, about 15 minutes. Cool pepper puree.

Combine pepper puree, flour, egg, 1 tablespoon sesame oil and salt in food processor. Process until ball forms. If dough is too dry, add 2 to 3 drops water and continue processing 30 seconds. (Dough can also be made by hand.) Divide dough into 4 equal parts. Cover and let stand 1 hour.

Flatten 1 piece of dough (keep remainder covered), then fold into thirds. Turn pasta machine to widest setting and run dough through several times until smooth and velvety, folding before each run and dusting with flour if sticky. Adjust machine to next narrower setting. Run dough through machine without folding. Repeat narrowing rollers after each run until pasta is ¹⁄₁₆-inch thick, dusting with flour as necessary. Hang dough sheet on drying rack or place on kitchen towels. Repeat with remaining dough. Set aside until sheets look leathery and edges begin to curl, 10 to 30 minutes depending on dampness of dough. *Pasta must be cut at this point or dough will be too brittle.*

Run sheets through fettuccine blades of pasta machine (or cut by hand into ¼-inch-wide strips). Arrange pasta on towel, overlapping as little as possible, until ready to cook. (*Can be prepared 1 month ahead, wrapped tightly and frozen.*)

Add pasta to large amount of rapidly boiling salted water, stirring to prevent sticking. Cook until just tender but firm to bite, about 1 minute. Drain and transfer to large bowl. Add oils, zucchini, green onions and sesame seeds.

For dressing: Combine all ingredients in blender or food processor and mix well. Pour 1½ cups dressing over noodles and toss to coat. Serve salad at room temperature. Just before serving, pour remaining dressing over noodles and toss.

Salad can be prepared 8 hours ahead, covered and refrigerated. Bring to room temperature before serving.

Fried Egg Noodles with Beef and Shrimp

2 servings

4 ounces fine egg noodles

1 medium onion, very thinly sliced and separated into rings
2 tablespoons all purpose flour
1/3 cup vegetable oil

2 tablespoons vegetable oil
3 shallots, minced
3 ounces beef or pork fillet, cut into julienne
4 medium-size uncooked shrimp, peeled and deveined

2 garlic cloves, minced
2 cabbage leaves, halved lengthwise and cut crosswise into thin strips
1 small carrot, peeled and sliced
1 ounce bean sprouts
3 green onions, thinly sliced
2 tablespoons soy sauce
Salt and freshly ground pepper
Minced fresh parsley

Cook noodles in rapidly boiling salted water until just tender but firm to bite. Drain; rinse noodles under cold water and drain thoroughly.

Toss onion in flour. Heat 1/3 cup oil in heavy 10-inch skillet over medium-high heat. Add onion and fry until golden brown and crisp, about 5 minutes. Remove with slotted spoon; drain on paper towels. Keep warm.

Heat 2 tablespoons oil in wok or heavy large skillet over medium-high heat. Add shallots and stir 1 minute. Add beef, shrimp and garlic and stir 2 minutes. Add cabbage and carrot and stir 4 minutes. Add noodles and bean sprouts and stir 3 minutes. Add green onions and soy sauce and cook until onions are heated through. Season with salt and pepper. Turn into bowl. Garnish with fried onion and parsley and serve immediately.

Grilled Beef with Noodles and Vegetables

6 servings

2 large sirloin strip steaks (1 1/3 pounds total), trimmed

4 large garlic cloves
6 tablespoons soy sauce
3 tablespoons honey
8 teaspoons sugar
8 teaspoons oriental sesame oil
8 teaspoons oyster sauce

3 ounces rice vermicelli

1 small unpeeled cucumber (10 ounces), scored and cut into feed-tube lengths

3 small onions (9 ounces total)
1 quart vegetable oil (for deep frying)

12 leaves green leaf lettuce, thick center ribs removed
2 medium tomatoes (10 ounces total), cored and sliced
1 1/2 cups bean sprouts

12 fresh mint sprigs
1 jalapeño chili, thinly sliced

Line baking sheet with waxed paper. Cut meat across grain to fit processor feed tube. Set meat on sheet. Freeze until just firm but still easily pierced with tip of sharp knife. (*Can be prepared 1 month ahead. Wrap tightly and return to freezer. Let thaw in refrigerator just until easily pierced with sharp knife.*)

With machine running, drop garlic through processor feed tube and mince. Add soy sauce, honey, sugar, sesame oil and oyster sauce and blend 3 seconds. Leave marinade in bowl.

Arrange meat in feed tube with grain perpendicular to thick slicer disc. Slice using firm pressure. Transfer beef mixture to large plastic bag. Marinate 6 hours or overnight, turning bag occasionally.

Place vermicelli in 3-quart bowl. Cover with boiling water. Let soak 20 minutes to soften. Drain thoroughly. Cut vermicelli into thirds (*Can be prepared 3 days ahead and refrigerated.*)

Stand cucumber in feed tube and slice with thin slicer, using medium pressure. Remove from work bowl. Stand onions in feed tube and slice using firm pressure. Heat oil in wok or large saucepan to 375°F. Add onions and fry until crisp, stirring occasionally, 2 to 3 minutes. Remove with slotted spoon and drain on paper towels.

Place 2 lettuce leaves on one half of each plate, with overlapping slices of cucumber and tomato, separated by a cluster of bean sprouts. Arrange ½ cup vermicelli on other half of plate.

Preheat broiler. Line jelly roll pan with foil. Arrange beef in single layer on pan. Pour marinade over. Broil beef 8 inches from heat source until no longer pink, about 2 minutes. Place atop vermicelli. Spoon pan juices over. Garnish plates with fried onions, mint and jalapeño slices. Serve hot.

For variation, ingredients can be rolled in 8-inch Vietnamese rice paper wrappers (banh trang). Fill jelly roll pan with hot water. Place 12 rice paper rounds in water, pressing edges down. Let soak 15 seconds. Drain. Set 1 lettuce leaf on each. Arrange fillings atop lettuce. Bring botton flap up and fold in 2 side flaps. Roll up tightly.

Mee Krob

A festive Thai first course from Los Angeles's Chan Dara restaurant.

6 appetizer servings

6 ounces rice stick noodles (mai fun)
Oil for deep frying

1 teaspoon vegetable oil
3 eggs, beaten to blend

9 tablespoons sugar
½ cup distilled white vinegar
6 tablespoons vegetable oil
3 tablespoons catsup

3 tablespoons fish sauce (nam pla)
1½ teaspoons paprika
8 ounces skinned and boned chicken, cut into ½-inch pieces
8 ounces uncooked medium shrimp, peeled and deveined
Bean sprouts, shredded green onion, cilantro sprigs and orange slices

Cut noodles at folds. Heat oil for deep frying in wok or heavy large skillet to 450°F. Sprinkle noodles lightly with water. Add to oil and fry until puffed and light brown on bottom, about 15 seconds. Turn and cook second side until light brown, about 15 seconds. Drain in paper towel-lined colander.

Heat 1 teaspoon oil in another heavy large skillet over medium-high heat. Pour in eggs, swirling pan to spread evenly. Cook until top is set, about 1 minute. Turn and cook second side until set, about 30 seconds. Transfer to work surface. Cool slightly, then cut omelet into ¼ × 1-inch pieces.

Combine sugar, vinegar, 6 tablespoons oil, catsup, fish sauce and paprika in wok or heavy large skillet over high heat. Boil until syrupy, stirring frequently, about 4 minutes. Add chicken and shrimp and stir until just firm to touch, about 1½ minutes. Cool 1 minute. Add noodles and omelet and mix gently until well coated. Transfer to platter and garnish with bean sprouts, green onion, cilantro and orange. Serve immediately.

Pancit with Pork and Prawns

4 to 6 servings

1 6³/₄-ounce package rice stick
  noodles (mai fun)
2 tablespoons vegetable oil
1 small onion, sliced
2 small garlic cloves, sliced
8 ounces boneless pork loin steaks,
  cut into thin strips
½ medium tomato, sliced
1 cup chopped cabbage

½ teaspoon freshly ground pepper
1 cup hot water
½ cup soy sauce
12 prawns, peeled, deveined and cut
  into thirds
2 hard-cooked eggs, sliced
2 green onions, sliced
  Paprika

Combine rice stick noodles in medium bowl with enough cold water to cover. Heat oil in large skillet over medium-high heat. Add onion and garlic and sauté until tender, about 1 minute. Stir in pork and sauté until no longer pink, about 3 minutes. Add tomato. Reduce heat to medium and cook 10 minutes. Drain noodles and add to pork with cabbage and pepper. Increase heat to medium-high. Mix in hot water and soy sauce. Cook until almost all liquid is absorbed and noodles are tender, about 7 minutes. Add prawns and cook until just pink, about 2 minutes. Garnish with eggs and green onions. Sprinkle with paprika. Serve immediately.

Japanese Noodle Salad

6 servings

½ ounce (about 6) dried shiitake
  mushrooms
8 ounces Japanese-style water
  noodles (udon)
3 tablespoons oriental sesame oil
3 tablespoons Japanese soy sauce
1 tablespoon rice vinegar or
  to taste

¼ teaspoon crushed dried red
  pepper flakes
2 tablespoons chopped green onion
1 tablespoon chopped cilantro
  (optional)

Soak mushrooms in warm water 1 hour. Squeeze to remove water; discard stems and thinly slice caps. Cook noodles in boiling salted water just until al dente. Drain and rinse with cold water. Combine mushrooms, oil, soy sauce, vinegar and pepper flakes in same pan used for noodles and warm through over medium heat. Add noodles, toss to coat and cook just until heated through. Garnish with green onion and cilantro.

Mee Siam

4 servings

Coconut Milk Sauce
2 tablespoons dried tamarind *or* fresh lemon juice

4 cups coconut milk
6 tablespoons Spice Paste*

1 pound rice stick noodles (mai fun)

Vegetable oil for deep frying
1 14-ounce package firm bean curd, drained

Lemon leaves
2 tablespoons vegetable oil
1 pound medium shrimp, peeled and deveined
6 tablespoons Spice Paste
1 pound bean sprouts
1 bunch green onions, slivered
3 hard-cooked eggs, quartered
2 limes, quartered

For sauce: If using tamarind, soak in ¾ cup warm water 5 minutes. Strain tamarind, reserving soaking liquid. Press on pulp to extract as much liquid as possible. Discard tamarind pulp.

Bring coconut milk and 6 tablespoons spice paste to boil in heavy medium saucepan over low heat, stirring constantly. Mix in tamarind soaking liquid (or lemon juice). Reduce heat and simmer 2 minutes, stirring constantly. Cool sauce completely.

Soak rice stick noodles in hot water to cover 5 minutes. Drain thoroughly.

Heat oil in deep fryer or another medium saucepan to 375°F. Add bean curd and fry until golden brown, about 5 minutes. Drain on paper towels. Slice bean curd thinly.

Line large platter with lemon leaves. Heat 1 tablespoon oil in wok or heavy deep skillet over high heat. Add shrimp and stir until just opaque, about 2 minutes. Transfer to plate using slotted spoon. Tent with foil to keep warm. Heat 1 tablespoon oil in wok set over high heat. Mix in 6 tablespoons spice paste. Add bean sprouts and stir 1 minute. Mix in half of cooked shrimp and half of green onions. Add noodles, 1 handful at a time, stirring until well mixed and heated through. Transfer to prepared platter. Garnish with remaining shrimp, green onions, bean curd, eggs and lime. Serve immediately, passing sauce separately.

*Spice Paste

Makes about ¾ cup

10 dried red chilies, seeded and cut into ½-inch pieces

1 medium onion, chopped
1 fresh lemongrass stalk, peeled and cut into 1-inch pieces, or 1 strip lemon peel
2 tablespoons crushed salted soya beans or soy sauce

1 teaspoon dried shrimp paste or anchovy paste
3 tablespoons vegetable oil
1 tablespoon sugar
1 teaspoon salt

Cover chilies with boiling water. Let stand 10 minutes. Drain off liquid.

Puree chilies, onion, lemongrass, soya beans and shrimp paste in processor. Heat oil in wok or heavy large skillet over low heat. Add pureed mixture and stir until aromatic, about 3 minutes. Add sugar and salt and stir 1 minute. Store in refrigerator.

Western-style Stir-fry in Rice Stick Nest

Begin with egg drop soup and round off the proceedings with lichee nuts.

4 servings

1 pound chicken breasts, boned, skinned and cut into ¹/₂-inch cubes
8 ounces jumbo shrimp, peeled and halved vertically
1 egg white
1 tablespoon cider vinegar
1 tablespoon cornstarch

1 large garlic clove, minced
1 teaspoon minced fresh ginger
1 cup jícama cut into thin sticks *or* 1 cup thinly sliced water chestnuts

10 snow peas, strings removed
¹/₂ cup fresh bean sprouts
¹/₂ cup bamboo shoots cut into thin sticks
1 small zucchini, cut into thin rounds

¹/₂ cup rich chicken stock
2¹/₂ tablespoons vinegar
1 tablespoon hoisin sauce
1 tablespoon cornstarch
¹/₈ to ¹/₄ teaspoon cayenne pepper
¹/₄ cup coarsely chopped salted cashews
2 green onions, minced
1 firm-ripe avocado, peeled, pitted and chopped
Juice of ¹/₂ lemon

3 cups vegetable oil for frying
3 ounces rice stick noodles (mai fun)

Salt

Marinate first 5 ingredients in refrigerator 1 hour, stirring occasionally.

Combine garlic and ginger on piece of waxed paper. Combine next 5 ingredients on another piece of waxed paper.

Mix stock, vinegar, hoisin, cornstarch and cayenne in measuring cup. Combine nuts and onion in bowl. Toss avocado with lemon juice and add to nuts.

Heat oil in wok to 390°F. Drop in half of noodles; they should puff immediately. Remove quickly with slotted spoon and drain on paper towels. Repeat with remaining noodles. Arrange around edge of ovenproof serving platter, leaving space in center. Keep warm.

Pour off all but 3 tablespoons oil from wok and reserve. Reheat oil in wok over high heat. Add chicken-shrimp mixture and stir-fry until chicken is barely firm, about 2 to 3 minutes. Remove from wok and keep warm.

Add 3 tablespoons reserved oil to wok and heat again over high heat. Add garlic and ginger and stir-fry until they begin to color, about 10 seconds. Add vegetable mixture and stir-fry until crisp-tender, about 2 minutes. Sprinkle with salt. Add stock and boil until liquid is thickened and clear, about 30 seconds. Return chicken and shrimp to wok and cook about 10 seconds. Turn into center of platter, top with cashew mixture and serve immediately.

Rice Noodle Salad with Chinese Sausage, Eggplant and Basil

Prepare all ingredients early in the day, then toss together just before serving.

4 servings

1 7-ounce Japanese eggplant, cut into 2 × 1/8-inch julienne
Salt

4 quarts boiling water
8 ounces 1/8-inch-thick Thai rice noodles

1/2 cup unsalted chicken stock
1/4 cup rice vinegar
1/4 cup light soy sauce
1 tablespoon wasabi (Japanese green horseradish powder)
1/2 teaspoon sugar

5 Chinese sausages (lop cheong)

5 tablespoons vegetable oil
2 large garlic cloves, cut into 1/8-inch cubes
Freshly ground pepper

2/3 cup chopped green onion
1/3 cup broken salted cashews
14 large basil leaves, thinly sliced
12 oak-leaf or other small lettuce leaves

Sprinkle eggplant lightly with salt. Spread between paper towels. Weight with cutting board or heavy baking pan. Let stand 1 hour.

Pour 4 quarts boiling water over noodles in large bowl. Cover noodles with towel and let stand until just tender but firm to bite, 6 to 9 minutes.

Meanwhile, combine stock, vinegar, soy sauce, wasabi and sugar in medium bowl. Rinse noodles with hot water. Drain well. Toss with sauce. Chill at least 4 hours, tossing occasionally.

Bring water to boil in bottom of steamer. Pierce sausages with fork and set on steamer rack. Cover and steam 10 minutes. Pierce sausages again and steam until cooked through, about 5 minutes. Cool. Slice thinly on diagonal. Pat with paper towels.

Heat 2 tablespoons oil in heavy large skillet over low heat. Add garlic and cook until golden brown, stirring occasionally, about 10 minutes. Transfer to platter using slotted spoon. Heat remaining 3 tablespoons oil in same skillet over high heat. Add eggplant and stir-fry until beginning to brown and crisp, about 5 minutes. Season with pepper. Add to garlic.

Drain most of dressing from noodles. Add sausages, eggplant and garlic, green onion, cashews and basil to noodles. Toss to blend. Adjust seasoning. Place 3 lettuce leaves in cluster on side of each plate. Mound noodle salad in center of plates and serve.

4 🍃 Vegetables, Salads and Condiments

The quest of harmony is expressed in every aspect of oriental culture, and nowhere is it more conspicuous than at the table. A carefully chosen menu, balancing flavors, textures and colors, creates an atmosphere that will be remembered long after the guests have gone. The entrée may be the center of attention, but the accompaniments, too, must be artful if the whole composition is to succeed.

Salads provide a cool counterpoint to spicy Asian dishes. A summer supper is the perfect time for refreshing Malaysian Rujak Salad (page 55), a blend of fresh pineapple, papaya and crisp vegetables in lime and tamarind juice. Indonesian Urap Salad with Grated Coconut (page 56) can help temper even the hottest entrée and is a natural at an Asian buffet. And easy-to-prepare Radish and Cucumber Relish (page 57) is a pleasant alternative to a lettuce salad.

Some vegetable dishes serve equally well as meatless entrées or accompaniments. Eggplant Hunan Style (page 47) stands well on its own, a zesty combination of fresh eggplant and pungent seasonings stir-fried for maximum flavor. From the kitchens of Shanghai comes Vegetarian Ten Mix (page 51), a colorful medley of vegetables and mushrooms stir-fried with oyster sauce, then sprinkled with a touch of sesame oil. Looking for a new twist at brunch? Slice a variety of fresh tropical fruits and serve them with crisp, golden-brown Batter-fried Plantain (page 50).

Pickled Green Papaya (page 57) typifies the do-ahead convenience of many accompaniments: This tangy papaya and bell pepper condiment can be made up to a month ahead. Pickled Vegetables with Oranges (page 58), also do-ahead, combines crisp green beans and snow peas with cool orange slices; it is delightful at a Chinese-style picnic.

And remember that most oriental dishes benefit by a simple, graceful garnish. The adornment may be as pristine as a pretty leaf or a carrot curl—or, for a lovely yet uncomplicated flourish, try Japanese Pickled Turnip Flowers (page 58), in which turnips are transformed into delicate pink "flowers." Even such simple means as these make any dinner seem a mandarin's feast.

 Vegetables

Hot and Spicy Szechwan Bean Curd

4 to 6 servings

2 tablespoons vegetable oil
6 ounces ground pork
  (about ¾ cup)
1 teaspoon minced garlic
⅔ cup chicken stock
¼ cup Chinese rice wine or
  dry Sherry
1 tablespoon light soy sauce
1½ teaspoons dark soy sauce
1¼ pounds tofu, rinsed, patted dry
  and cut into ½-inch dice

¼ cup Cornstarch Mixture
  (see page 66)
¼ cup sliced green onion tops
¼ cup red chili oil or to taste
Salt
1 tablespoon oriental sesame oil
¼ teaspoon roasted and ground
  Szechwan pepper*
Freshly cooked rice

Heat vegetable oil in wok over high heat. Add pork and garlic and stir-fry until pork begins to lose pink color, about 30 seconds. Mix in stock, rice wine and both soy sauces. Add bean curd and toss. Reduce heat, cover and simmer only until meat is cooked through, stirring occasionally, about 3 minutes. Add cornstarch mixture, green onion, chili oil and salt. Stir until sauce thickens slightly. Mix in sesame oil. Transfer to heated platter. Sprinkle top with Szechwan pepper. Serve immediately with rice.

*Roast Szechwan peppercorns in heavy dry skillet over medium-low heat until aromatic, about 3 minutes. Grind finely.

Chinese Bean Curd with Chili-Garlic Paste

10 buffet servings

1½ cups degreased chicken stock
1½ pounds whole fresh bean curd
¼ cup dried tree ears, softened in
  hot water and drained

¼ cup vegetable oil
6 green onions, minced
1 3-inch piece fresh ginger, minced
2 tablespoons chili paste with
  garlic or to taste

2 tablespoons oriental sesame oil
1 teaspoon salt
8 ounces fresh or frozen lima
  beans, cooked until tender,
  drained and cooled
Alfafa sprouts

Bring stock to boil in medium skillet. Reduce heat so broth barely shimmers. Add bean curd and poach 1 minute. Remove from skillet using slotted spoon. Cut into 1-inch cubes. Blanch tree ears in stock 30 seconds. Drain; remove hard cores. Reserve stock.

Heat oil in wok or heavy large skillet over medium-high heat. Add onions and ginger and fry until fragrant, about 30 seconds. Remove from heat. Blend in chili paste, sesame oil, salt and reserved stock. Combine bean curd, tree ears and lima beans in large bowl. Mix dressing in gently. Arrange bed of alfafa sprouts on large platter. Top with bean curd mixture and serve.

Eggplant Hunan Style

*A spectrum of flavors—
sour, salty, sweet, fragrant
and hot.*

6 servings

6 tablespoons peanut oil
1 1½-pound eggplant, cut into
   1-inch chunks (unpeeled)
3 garlic cloves, minced
1 tablespoon chili paste with garlic
1½ teaspoons minced fresh ginger

½ cup chicken stock
1 tablespoon soy sauce
2 teaspoons sugar
1 tablespoon rice vinegar
2 tablespoons chopped green onion
1 teaspoon oriental sesame oil

Heat 4 tablespoons peanut oil in heavy 12-inch skillet over medium heat. Add eggplant and stir-fry until soft, about 3 minutes. Remove using slotted spoon; set aside. Add remaining 2 tablespoons peanut oil to skillet and warm over medium heat. Add garlic, chili paste and cook 15 seconds. Add stock, soy sauce and sugar and bring to boil. Add vinegar and eggplant and cook until eggplant has absorbed most of sauce, about 1 minute. Stir in green onion and sesame oil. Serve hot, removing eggplant with slotted spoon.

Japanese Spicy Eggplant (Nasu Itame-Ni)

8 servings

1½ pounds eggplant (about 8 small
   Japanese eggplants or
   1 large eggplant)
½ cup (about) vegetable oil
2 dried hot red peppers

4 tablespoons Japanese soy sauce
2 tablespoons tahini
1 tablespoon mirin (syrupy rice
   wine) or dry Sherry

If using small eggplants, remove stem end, halve lengthwise and make diagonal slashes about 1 inch apart halfway through eggplant. Cut in half crosswise. If using large eggplant, cut into pieces about 2½ inches by ½ inch; do not peel. Cut diagonal slashes about 1 inch apart as for small eggplants.

Heat several tablespoons oil in skillet or wok over medium-high heat. Add red peppers and eggplant and stir-fry 2 to 3 minutes, adding more oil if necessary (use as little as possible).

Arrange eggplant and peppers in steamer and sprinkle with 2 tablespoons soy sauce. Steam until tender, about 10 minutes. Combine tahini with remaining 2 tablespoons soy sauce and mirin. Discard peppers. Arrange eggplant on salad plates. Top each serving with sesame mixture.

Sesame Stir-fried Mushrooms

*An interesting oriental
appetizer or side dish.*

Makes 2 cups

1 ounce dried shiitake mushrooms
3 tablespoons unsalted butter
3 tablespoons peanut oil or
   vegetable oil

½ teaspoon oriental sesame oil
8 ounces mushrooms, sliced
¼ cup sesame seeds
3 tablespoons dark soy sauce

Soak dried mushrooms in small bowl in enough warm water to cover for 30 minutes. Drain; squeeze out excess liquid. Remove stems and discard. Cut caps into ½-inch slices. Heat butter and oils in large skillet over medium-high heat. When very hot, add dried and fresh mushrooms and cook 3 minutes, shaking pan constantly. Add sesame seeds and soy sauce and continue cooking until heated through. Serve hot or at room temperature.

Stir-fry of Zucchini, Pepper and Celery

12 servings

4 to 5 tablespoons peanut oil
4 cups ½-inch-thick slices celery
8 to 10 medium zucchini, cut into ½-inch-thick slices
6 red bell peppers, cut into ½-inch-wide strips

½ cup snipped fresh chives
4 teaspoons freshly ground pepper
2 teaspoons minced fresh oregano or ½ teaspoon dried, crumbled
Salt
Chopped fresh parsley (garnish)

Heat oil in heavy large skillet over medium-high heat. Add celery and stir-fry until barely tender. Add zucchini and peppers and stir-fry until barely tender. Stir in chives, pepper and oregano with salt to taste and cook 1 more minute. Top with parsley and serve.

Parmesan Tempura

Traditional tempura with a twist.

6 servings

2 small zucchini, cut into very fine 2-inch-long julienne
Salt

4 cups vegetable oil
1 egg
10 tablespoons unbleached all purpose flour
½ cup freshly grated Parmesan cheese

1 cup ice water
Pinch of freshly ground pepper
3 small carrots, peeled and thinly sliced on diagonal
20 spinach leaves, stemmed
1 squid, cleaned and sliced into ¼-inch-thick rings
12 sea scallops, halved
Nasturtium flowers and leaves

Sprinkle zucchini lightly with salt. Layer between paper towels. Weight with cutting board. Let stand 6 hours.

Heat oil to 370°F in wok or deep fryer. Preheat oven to 170°F (or lowest setting). Blend egg in medium bowl, using fork. Lightly blend in flour, cheese, ice water and pepper; mixture will be lumpy. Dip small clusters of zucchini in batter; drain. Add zucchini to oil in batches (do not crowd) and fry until light brown, turning occasionally, about 3 minutes. Drain on paper towels. Arrange in single layer on baking sheet lined with paper towels. Keep warm in oven. Repeat with carrots and spinach, skimming oil occasionally. Pat squid and scallops dry. Dip in batter and fry in batches. Sprinkle tempura with salt if desired. Transfer to napkin-lined basket. Garnish with flowers and serve immediately.

Asparagus Tempura

8 appetizer servings

2 cups ice water
1⅔ cups all purpose flour
1 egg yolk
⅛ teaspoon baking soda

3 cups vegetable oil
2 pounds thin raw asparagus, trimmed
Salt

Combine first 4 ingredients in medium mixing bowl and beat until smooth. Cover and refrigerate until ready to use.

To prepare, heat oil in wok or shallow pan to 375°F. Dip asparagus in batter and fry in batches until golden brown. Drain on paper towels, salt lightly and serve immediately.

Mandarin Pancakes with Chinois Vegetable Filling

Classically, two Mandarin pancakes are cooked back to back for expediency and then peeled apart before filling. Accompany with hoisin sauce.

6 servings

Mandarin Pancakes
2 cups (or more) all purpose flour
¼ teaspoon salt
1 cup boiling water
1 tablespoon sesame oil

All purpose flour
Sesame oil (about 1 tablespoon)

Chinois Vegetable Filling
1 ounce shiitake mushrooms*
½ ounce cloud ear mushrooms*

2 tablespoons (¼ stick) butter
3 ounces snow peas, ends trimmed
and strings removed

2 tablespoons (¼ stick) butter
¼ cup minced green onion
2 teaspoons minced fresh ginger
1½ pounds Napa cabbage,
thinly sliced
1⅓ cups whipping cream
1 tablespoon fresh lemon juice or
to taste
Salt and freshly ground pepper or
Szechwan pepper

For pancakes: Combine 2 cups flour with salt in bowl. Add boiling water and 1 tablespoon sesame oil and stir with fork or wooden spoon until flour is moistened. Set aside until cool enough to handle, about 5 minutes. Turn dough out onto lightly floured surface and knead until smooth and elastic, about 7 minutes, adding more flour if dough is sticky.

Divide dough into 12 equal pieces. Dust both sides lightly with flour and pat into 3-inch circles. Brush 6 circles generously with sesame oil, moistening edges well. Place remaining 6 circles on top of oiled circles, stretching as necessary so edges meet. Roll out on lightly floured surface, turning circles over occasionally, until 8 inches in diameter.

Heat heavy ungreased skillet (preferably cast iron) over medium heat. Add pancakes one at a time and cook until puffed and dried on top and speckled medium brown on bottom, about 2 minutes. Turn and cook until second side is speckled, about 1 minute. Immediately find seam at edge and gently peel pancakes apart. Stack pancakes and wrap in aluminum foil; set aside.

For filling: Combine mushrooms in small bowl with enough hot water to cover and let stand until softened, about 30 minutes. Squeeze dry; discard hard stems. Slice caps thinly.

Melt 2 tablespoons butter in heavy large skillet over medium-high heat. Add snow peas and stir-fry until crisp-tender, about 3 minutes. Remove from skillet. Snip peas in half crosswise with scissors.

Melt 2 tablespoons butter in same skillet over low heat. Add green onion and ginger and cook, stirring, until onion is transparent, about 3 minutes. Add cabbage, increase heat to medium-high and stir-fry until wilted, about 3 minutes. Stir in mushrooms and cream. Bring to boil, reduce heat and simmer until liquid is absorbed, stirring occasionally. Add lemon juice. Season to taste with salt and pepper. (*Can be prepared ahead to this point and set aside.*)

To serve, steam wrapped pancakes over boiling water until heated through (or rewarm in oven), about 15 minutes. Meanwhile, place filling over medium-high heat. Add snow peas and stir briefly just to heat through; do not overcook. Spoon filling onto nonbrowned side of hot pancakes. Roll up crepe style. Arrange pancakes seam side down on heated platter and serve immediately.

*An equal amount of any other type of dried mushroom can be substituted.

Chinese Eggplant with Garlic Sauce

8 servings

1 10- to 12-ounce piece pork tenderloin, well trimmed and cut into matchsticks (freeze 30 minutes before slicing)
1 tablespoon dry Sherry or Chinese rice wine
½ egg white
 Pinch of salt
1 tablespoon cornstarch

Sauce

6 tablespoons chicken stock
2½ tablespoons soy sauce
1½ tablespoons vinegar
1½ tablespoons sugar
1 tablespoon cornstarch dissolved in 1 tablespoon water

1 tablespoon chili paste with garlic
1 tablespoon dry Sherry or Chinese rice wine

4 cups vegetable oil
1 12-ounce eggplant, peeled and cut into finger-size strips

1 tablespoon vegetable oil
½ green bell pepper, cut into 2 × ⅙-inch strips
½ red bell pepper, cut into 2 × ⅙-inch strips
1 tablespoon minced fresh ginger
1 teaspoon minced fresh garlic
⅓ cup diced green onion
½ teaspoon oriental sesame oil

Place pork in mixing bowl. Add Sherry, egg white and salt and mix with hands until egg white is foamy. Add cornstarch and mix again until smooth. Cover and refrigerate at least 1 hour.

For sauce: Combine stock, soy sauce, vinegar, sugar, dissolved cornstarch, chili paste and Sherry in small bowl and mix well; set aside.

Heat 4 cups oil in wok or deep fryer to 350°F. Add eggplant in small batches and fry until lightly colored. Drain between paper towels, pressing to remove as much oil as possible.

Let same oil cool down to 280°F. Add pork and stir constantly until pieces separate. Cook 1 minute longer. Let drain in sieve. (*Can be done 6 to 8 hours ahead to this point and refrigerated.*)

Heat 1 tablespoon oil in wok or large skillet over high heat. Add peppers, ginger and garlic and stir-fry 10 to 15 seconds. Add eggplant, pork and sauce (stir before adding) and stir gently until heated through and sauce is bubbling and thickened. Stir in green onion. Remove from heat and stir in sesame oil. Serve immediately.

Batter-fried Plantain (Pisang Goreng)

Substitute these for pan-cakes at your next brunch.

6 servings

2 to 3 tablespoons milk
1 egg
1 tablespoon firmly packed brown sugar
6 tablespoons all purpose flour
 Pinch of salt

Corn oil for frying
1 large or 2 medium-size ripe plantains* (with almost black skin), peeled and cut diagonally into ½-inch-thick slices

Mix milk, egg, sugar, flour and salt until smooth. Heat oil in large skillet over medium heat. Dip each plantain slice into batter, then drop into oil. Fry until browned, about 2 minutes on each side. Drain on paper towel. Serve warm or at room temperature.

*Bananas can be substituted; halve horizontally instead of slicing.

Vegetarian Ten Mix

All ingredients for this mélange can be found at oriental markets

4 main-course servings or 6 servings as part of multi-course Chinese meal

24 golden needles (dried lily buds)
12 small cloud ears
6 small Chinese dried black mushrooms
1 ounce dried bean curd sheets, broken into 2-inch pieces
¼ teaspoon baking soda

2 tablespoons water
1½ teaspoons cornstarch
1½ teaspoons oyster sauce

3 tablespoons vegetable oil
2 medium carrots, peeled and thinly sliced
4 ounces bok choy (green leaves with ½ inch stem), cut into ½-inch pieces

3 ounces canned vegetarian mock abalone or canned fried gluten
6 ears canned baby corn, halved lengthwise
2½ ounces canned straw mushrooms, drained
1 ounce canned bamboo shoot, rinsed and thinly sliced
2 tablespoons chicken stock seasoned with salt and pepper
1 teaspoon salt
½ teaspoon oriental sesame oil

Cover golden needles and cloud ears with boiling water and soak to soften, about 30 minutes. Soak black mushrooms in bowl of lukewarm water to cover to soften, about 25 minutes. Bring small saucepan of water to boil. Remove from heat. Stir in bean curd and baking soda. Soak 10 minutes.

Rinse golden needles and cloud ears and drain. Discard stems from black mushrooms. Rinse mushrooms and squeeze out excess moisture. Rinse bean curd and drain thoroughly.

Combine 2 tablespoons water with cornstarch and oyster sauce.

Heat wok or heavy large skillet over high heat 1 minute. Add oil and heat 30 seconds. Add black mushrooms and carrots and stir 2 minutes. Add bok choy and toss 1 minute. Add remaining vegetables, stock and salt. Stir-fry 3 minutes. Stir oyster sauce mixture and add to wok. Stir-fry until sauce thickens and coats vegetables, about 2 minutes. Transfer mixture to deep platter. Sprinkle with sesame oil. Serve vegetables immediately.

 Salads

Japanese Cucumber Salad with Sweet Vinegar Dressing (Kyuri-Momi)

6 servings

3 cucumbers, peeled, seeded and thinly sliced, or 3 daikon (Japanese white radishes), thinly sliced
1 tablespoon salt

½ cup rice vinegar
6 tablespoons sugar
Enoki mushrooms (optional garnish)

Place cucumber or daikon in colander and sprinkle with salt. Let stand 30 minutes. Rinse, drain and pat dry. Transfer to bowl Add vinegar and sugar and mix well. Chill thoroughly. Garnish with mushrooms if desired.

Japanese Vinegared Broccoli Salad (Su No Mono)

4 servings

1 pound broccoli

Dressing
½ cup rice vinegar

1 tablespoon sugar
¼ teaspoon dry mustard

4 radish roses

Divide broccoli into florets. Trim stalks to 1 inch. (Save remaining stalks for another use.) Bring large pot of salted water to rapid boil over high heat. Add broccoli and cook until crisp-tender, 5 to 6 minutes. Drain and rinse under cold running water. Drain well and pat dry with paper towels. Refrigerate.

For dressing: Combine vinegar, sugar and mustard in small bowl and blend.

Arrange broccoli on 4 salad plates. Spoon dressing over top. Garnish each serving with radish rose.

Mrs. Fan's Cabbage Salad

This crisp, piquant relish always starts the dinner at Auntie Yuan, a celebrated "nouvelle" Chinese restaurant in New York.

8 to 10 servings

1 12-ounce Napa cabbage, halved lengthwise, cored and shredded
½ cup loosely packed shredded green onions
¼ cup cilantro leaves
¼ cup oriental sesame oil
¼ cup fresh lemon juice

4½ teaspoons dried shrimp, rinsed and finely minced
1 tablespoon sugar
1 tablespoon distilled white vinegar
2 teaspoons minced garlic
¼ teaspoon salt or to taste

Combine all ingredients in large bowl. Cover and refrigerate 1 to 4 hours. Adjust seasoning just before serving.

Shanghai Radish Salad

2 to 4 appetizer servings

10 ounces Chinese white radish* or Japanese white radish (daikon), peeled and cut into
⅛ × 3-inch julienne
Salt
2 medium carrots, peeled and cut into ⅛ × 3-inch julienne

2½ teaspoons vegetable oil
1 small fresh jalapeño or other green chili, seeded and cut into
⅛ × 3-inch julienne

½ medium-size red bell pepper, seeded and cut into
⅛ × 3-inch julienne
1 tablespoon sugar
1 tablespoon distilled white vinegar

½ teaspoon oriental sesame oil

Toss radish with ¾ teaspoon salt in nonaluminum bowl. Toss carrots with pinch of salt in another bowl. Let stand 1 hour to draw off liquid

Heat wok or heavy large skillet over high heat 1 minute. Add vegetable oil and heat 45 seconds. Turn off heat and stir in jalapeño and bell peppers to coat with oil. Mix in sugar and vinegar. Let cool in wok 5 minutes.

Squeeze excess liquid from radish and carrots. Combine in bowl. Stir in pepper mixture and sesame oil. Refrigerate 1½ hours to develop flavors.

Drain off any liquid. Arrange radish salad on platter and serve.

*Chinese white radish, a vegetable about 8 inches long and 3 inches in diameter, is also called Chinese turnip or giant white radish.

Chinese Cucumber Salad

2 to 6 appetizer servings

1 pound cucumbers, peeled, halved
   lengthwise and seeded
¾ teaspoon salt

1 tablespoons distilled
   white vinegar
2 teaspoons sugar

Cut cucumbers crosswise into ¹/₁₀-inch-thick slices. Toss with salt in nonaluminum bowl. Let stand 1 hour.

Drain cucumbers thoroughly. Return to bowl and toss with vinegar and sugar. Drain again. Arrange slices on platter and serve immediately.

Japanese Radish and Carrot Salad in Lemon Cups (Kohaku Namasu)

*Use as a first course
or garnish.*

Makes 12 salad cups

6 small lemons

Rice vinegar
¼ cup sugar
¼ teaspoon salt

1½ cups julienne of peeled daikon
   (Japanese white radish)
Salt
¼ cup julienne of peeled carrot

Cut lemons in half. Squeeze juice into measuring cup. Scoop out pulp and discard, reserving lemon shells. Trim bottoms so halves stand upright. If using within 2 hours, stuff each with damp paper towels. (Cover with plastic and freeze if preparing ahead.)

Add enough vinegar to lemon juice to equal ½ cup. Transfer to small saucepan. Add sugar and ¼ teaspoon salt and cook over low heat just until sugar and salt dissolve. Remove sauce from heat, cover and refrigerate.

Place radish julienne in medium bowl. Sprinkle lightly with salt. Let stand 2 to 3 minutes. Squeeze to wilt slightly; drain well. (If radish is strongly flavored, soak in cold water 5 minutes and squeeze dry.) Repeat for carrot.

Combine carrot and radish in large bowl. Pour chilled lemon sauce over vegetables. (*Can be made 5 days ahead to this point, covered and refrigerated.*) Let stand at room temperature at least 30 minutes. To serve, drain vegetables well. Mound into lemon shells. Serve chilled or at room temperature.

Malaysian Spinach Salad with Spicy Dressing

*For best results, fry the
bean curd just before
serving the salad.*

4 to 6 servings

Spicy Dressing
1 tablespoon dried tamarind *or*
   fresh lemon juice

3 small fresh red chilies, seeded
1 teaspoon dried shrimp paste or
   anchovy paste
1 tablespoon firmly packed
   brown sugar
1 tablespoon fresh lime juice
1 tablespoon (or more) cold water
½ teaspoon salt
½ cup chunky peanut butter or
   ground roasted peanuts

4 ounces bean sprouts

Vegetable oil for deep frying
2 pieces firm bean curd

1 bunch spinach leaves
1 small cucumber, peeled and sliced
1 cup slightly underripe
   pineapple chunks
1 cup sliced water chestnuts

For dressing: If using tamarind, soak in ¼ cup water 5 minutes. Strain tamarind soaking liquid. Press on pulp to extract as much liquid as possible.

Finely grind chilies and shrimp paste in processor. Add tamarind soaking liquid (or lemon juice), sugar, lime juice, 1 tablespoon water and salt and blend. Add peanut butter and process until well combined. Mix in more water if dressing is too thick to pour.

Blanch bean sprouts in large pot of boiling water 30 seconds. Rinse under cold water; drain well.

Heat oil in deep fryer or large saucepan to 375°F. Add bean curd and fry until golden brown, about 5 minutes. Drain on paper towels. Slice thinly.

Combine bean sprouts, bean curd and all remaining ingredients in salad bowl. Add dressing, toss lightly, and serve.

Japanese Spinach with Sesame Dressing (Ae Mono)

8 servings

1 pound fresh spinach, stemmed

⅓ cup toasted sesame seeds
¼ cup Japanese soy sauce
1 tablespoon mirin (syrup rice wine) or dry Sherry

2 tablespoons sugar
8 fresh flowers (optional garnish)

Bring large pot of salted water to boil over high heat. Add spinach and cook 5 minutes. Drain into colander; rinse under cold running water. Gently squeeze dry with hands. Divide spinach evenly among 8 salad plates.

Lightly crush sesame seeds using mortar and pestle. Transfer to small bowl. Add soy sauce, mirin and sugar and blend until smooth. Spoon over spinach. Serve at room temperature or chilled. Garnish each with flower.

Japanese Spinach Bundles

4 to 6 servings

1 pound large spinach leaves (trim off all but about 2 inches of stem)

Dressing
2 tablespoons Japanese soy sauce
2 tablespoons white vinegar

2 tablespoons vegetable oil
1 tablespoon sugar
Salt
2 tablespoons toasted white sesame seeds

Bring large pot of salted water to rolling boil. Add spinach and let boil 1 minute. Drain thoroughly, rinse under cold running water and drain again.

Working with ¼ of spinach at a time, squeeze with hands to remove all moisture and shape into neat 2-inch bundles. Cut each in half crosswise and set cut side down on serving plate.

For dressing: Combine all ingredients except sesame seeds and mix well. Pour over spinach. Sprinkle with toasted sesame seeds before serving.

Thai Green Papaya Salad

6 servings

1 to 3 dried red chilies, seeded
   and chopped
1 garlic clove, peeled
8 ounces underripe papaya, peeled
   and shredded

3 tablespoons fresh lime juice
2 tablespoons fish sauce (nam pla)
1 head cabbage or
   iceberg lettuce, shredded
1 large tomato, sliced

Grind chilies and garlic in mortar with pestle. Transfer to large nonaluminum bowl. Mix in papaya, lime juice and fish sauce. Mound cabbage on platter. Top with papaya salad. Garnish with tomato and serve.

Watercress and Water Chestnut Salad

2 servings

½ bunch watercress (about
   2 ounces), tough stems discarded
2 ounces fresh water chestnuts or
   jícama, peeled and cut
   into julienne
4 radishes, coarsely grated

3 tablespoons vegetable oil
1 tablespoon fresh lemon juice
1 teaspoon oriental sesame oil
1 teaspoon toasted sesame seeds
   Salt and freshly ground pepper

Divide watercress between individual salad plates. Arrange water chestnuts or jícama in sunburst pattern over top. Place grated radishes in center.

    Combine all remaining ingredients in small jar and shake well. Pour over salads and serve immediately.

Malaysian Rujak Salad

*A good accompaniment
to spicy fare.*

10 buffet servings

2 cups fresh bean sprouts

½ cup tamarind juice
⅓ cup fresh lime juice
1 tablespoon sugar
   Dash of salt
1 small pineapple, peeled,
   quartered, cored and thinly sliced

1 small papaya, peeled, halved,
   seeded and thinly sliced
2 cups finely shredded cabbage
2 medium cucumbers, peeled,
   halved, seeded and thinly sliced
1 cup shredded lettuce leaves
   Slivers of fresh red chilies

Place bean sprouts in colander. Pour boiling water over to soften slightly.

    Blend tamarind juice, lime juice, sugar and salt. Arrange pineapple, papaya and cabbage in three-leaf clover pattern on shallow large platter. Top with bean sprouts, cucumbers and lettuce. Garnish with chilies. Spoon dressing over and serve immediately.

Chinese Vegetable Salad

4 to 6 servings

4 ounces snow peas,
strings removed
2 medium cucumbers, peeled,
halved, seeded and cut into
1/4-inch-thick slices
1 small celery stalk, peeled and cut
into 2-inch matchsticks

Chinese Salad Dressing
2 tablespoons vegetable oil

1 1/2 teaspoons chili paste with garlic
or to taste
1/4 cup light soy sauce
1/4 cup white vinegar
3 tablespoons oriental sesame oil
2 tablespoons firmly packed
brown sugar

Bring large pot of water to boil. Add snow peas and blanch 30 seconds. Drain, rinse under cold water and drain again. Combine with cucumber and celery in large serving bowl.

For dressing: Heat 2 tablespoons vegetable oil in small skillet. Add chili paste and stir-fry until heated. Add remaining ingredients and mix well.

One hour before serving, toss vegetables with dressing. Cover and refrigerate until serving time.

For variation, fresh broccoli, cut into 1- to 2-inch pieces, can be substituted for snow peas. Parboil 30 seconds and drain thoroughly.

Indonesian Urap Salad with Grated Coconut

10 buffet servings

4 cups shredded cabbage
2 large carrots, cut into
matchstick julienne
14 ounces green beans, cut into
matchstick julienne
2 cups fresh bean sprouts
1 cup bamboo shoots, cut
into strips

1/2 teaspoon shrimp paste (kapee)
1 cup minced onion

1 cup freshly grated or dried
shredded coconut
1/4 cup fresh lemon juice
1/4 cup water
1/4 teaspoon salt
1/4 teaspoon cayenne pepper or
to taste

Blanch cabbage, carrots and green beans separately in boiling salted water until amost crisp-tender. Drain well. Pour boiling water over bean sprouts and bamboo shoots in colander. Drain well, then pat dry.

Heat heavy large skillet over medium high heat. Add shrimp paste and stir until fragrant. Reduce heat to low. Add remaining ingredients and bring to simmer. Cool; dressing will be thick.

Combine vegetables in bowl. Mix in dressing. Serve at room temperature.

Shoji's House Dressing

Makes about 2 cups

3/4 cup vegetable oil
5 tablespoons minced onion
3 tablespoons rice vinegar
3 1/2 teaspoons soy sauce
3 1/2 teaspoons catsup
3 1/2 teaspoons water

1 1/2 teaspoons minced celery
1 teaspoon grated fresh ginger
1 teaspoon grated lemon peel
1/2 teaspoon salt
1/2 teaspoon freshly ground pepper

Combine all ingredients in blender and mix until smooth. Store dressing in tightly covered container in refrigerator.

*Top left and bottom right:
Kiku-Zushi (Chrysanthemum
Sushi with Red Caviar)
Top right: Maki Mono (Rolled
Sushi with Cucumber)
Center: Negi Maki (Beef and
Scallion Rolls)
Lower left: Konbu Maki (Kelp
Rolls with Gourd Ribbon)*

*Top, left to right: Lumpiang Sinkamas
(Crisp-fried Pork and Shrimp
Dumplings) and Crispy Chicken Skins
in bread sculpture
Bottom left: Papaya Achara (Pickled
Green Papaya)
Bottom right: Eggplant Dip*

Irwin Horowitz

*Clockwise from top left: Wasabi Paste;
two kinds of Sushi; Kyuri-Momi
(Cucumber Salad with Sweet Vinegar
Dressing); Kara-Age (Double-fried
Chicken with Ginger and Sesame Oil)*

Banh Xeo Saigon (Saigon Crepe)

Cha Gio (Spring Rolls)

Coconut Flan

Vegetarian Ten Mix

Brian Leatart

Tori No Matsukasa Ni ("Pinecone" Chicken Patties)
and Hana Kabu (Pickled Turnip Flowers)

Peter J. Kaplan

❦ Condiments

Radish and Cucumber Relish

6 servings

½ cup fresh parsley leaves
2 tablespoons sugar
1½ teaspoons salt
1 1-inch piece of
  fresh ginger, peeled
¾ cup rice vinegar

2 medium-size chilled cucumbers
  (1½ pounds total), unpeeled,

scored, cut in half lengthwise,
seeded and cut into lengths to fit
processor feed tube
24 large chilled red radishes
  (16 ounces total), trimmed
  Freshly ground white pepper

Mince parsley in processor using on/off turns. Transfer to small bowl and set aside. Add sugar and salt to work bowl. With machine running, drop ginger through feed tube and mix until finely minced. Pour in rice vinegar and blend 5 seconds.

Remove steel knife and insert thin or medium slicer. Place cucumber pieces vertically in feed tube and slice using medium pressure. Add radishes to feed tube and slice using firm pressure. Transfer vegetable mixture to 1½-quart salad bowl and toss gently. Taste and season with pepper. Sprinkle parsley over. Serve immediately.

Pickled Green Papaya (Papaya Achara)

This refreshing Philippine condiment must be started at least two days before serving.

12 servings

1 pound green papaya, peeled,
  seeded and cut into
  ⅛-inch julienne
1 large red bell pepper, seeded and
  cut into ⅛-inch julienne
1 large green bell pepper, seeded
  and cut into ⅛-inch julienne
1 cup rock salt

¼ cup slivered shallots
3 medium garlic cloves, slivered
2 tablespoons slivered fresh ginger

1⅓ cups distilled white vinegar

1 cup sugar
  Freshly ground pepper

Mix papaya, bell peppers, rock salt, shallots, garlic and ginger in large bowl. Cover mixture and marinate overnight at room temperature.

Drain papaya mixture. Rinse with cold water and drain again. Return to bowl. Mix in ⅔ cup vinegar. Marinate overnight at room temperature.

Drain papaya mixture. Rinse with cold water and drain. Heat sugar, remaining ⅔ cup vinegar and pepper in heavy small saucepan over low heat until sugar dissolves, swirling pan occasionally. Increase heat and bring to boil. Stir into papaya mixture. Cover and refrigerate at least 2 hours. Drain before serving. *Pickle can be stored in refrigerator up to 1 month.*

❦

Pickled Vegetables with Oranges

6 servings

8 ounces green beans (trimmed), halved crosswise

4 ounces snow peas, ends trimmed and strings removed

1¼ cups rice vinegar
1¼ cups water
½ cup sugar

2 dried red chilies, seeded
1 1-inch piece fresh ginger, very thinly sliced
½ teaspoon salt
1 small orange (4 ounces), very thinly sliced and seeded

Bring large amount of salted water to rapid boil over high heat. Add beans and cook until crisp-tender, about 5 to 6 minutes. Remove with slotted spoon and drain well. Rinse in cold water and drain again. Repeat with snow peas. Pat beans and snow peas dry.

Combine vinegar, water, sugar, chilies, ginger and salt in large saucepan over low heat and cook until sugar dissolves, swirling mixture occasionally. Increase heat and bring to boil Let boil 5 minutes. Add orange slices and let marinate until completely cool.

Pack beans, peas, ginger and orange slices evenly into 1-quart jar with tight-fitting lid. Pour in marinade. Refrigerate pickled vegetables for at least 1 day or up to 3 days before serving.

Japanese Pickled Turnip Flowers (Hana Kabu)

These tart and crisp "flowers" make lovely garnishes for roasts or poultry. Set the turnip between two chopsticks while cutting to help keep the vegetable more steady.

Makes 6 flowers

½ cup rice vinegar
¼ cup sugar
¼ teaspoon salt

6 small white turnips, peeled
2 teaspoons salt
5 to 6 aka-jiso no shio-zukē leaves or shiso sugata leaves (picked herb leaves), optional

1 to 2 tōgarashi (dried hot red peppers), optional
Chrysanthemum leaves (optional garnish)

Combine rice vinegar, sugar and ¼ teaspoon salt in small saucepan. Cook over low heat just until sugar and salt dissolve. Cover and refrigerate.

Trim small slice from bottom of turnip. Place turnip on work surface and cut thin vertical slices in turnip almost to bottom (be careful not to cut through). Turn turnip around and repeat slicing, forming crisscross pattern. Repeat for remaining turnips. Sprinkle turnips with salt. Let drain 5 minutes. Squeeze until slightly wilted. Rinse under cold water and squeeze dry. Fit turnips closely together in wide-mouthed glass jar. Fill with vinegar mixture. Add pickled herb leaves (for pink-purple shade) or dried red peppers (for spicy hot taste). Cover and let stand at room temperature at least 8 hours to marinate or refrigerate up to 3 months. To serve, drain turnips well. Arrange on serving platter. Press each "petal" lightly to open "flowers." Surround with chrysanthemum leaves.

5 ❦ Seafood

The Chinese mainland—not to mention such island nations as Taiwan, Japan and Indonesia—has vast stretches of coastline and countless rivers and streams. Generations have feasted on the fresh- and saltwater catch—which in many cases makes its way straight from the water into the wok.

Seafood must be cooked with care if its delicate texture is to be preserved. Undercooked pieces may be tough, while overdone fish tends to fall apart. This is why the oriental technique of stir-frying is perfect for seafood: Ingredients are cut into bite-size pieces, placed briefly in hot oil and stirred constantly to ensure quick, even cooking. Among the stir-fry recipes in this chapter are Philippine Prawns with Green Beans and Coconut (page 68), Coral Fish Slices (page 62) and Chinese Tofu Casserole (page 70), each of which combines fresh seafood with crisp vegetables and pungent seasonings.

Larger pieces of seafood may be steamed, gently absorbing the aroma of the savory steaming liquid. Traditionally, round, shallow baskets, often made from bamboo, were stacked so that the practical cook could steam several items simultaneously. Modern cooks can choose between basket steamers and aluminum models, or can improvise by placing the plate of food on a rack or inverted bowl in a large pot: Just add water to a level of two inches below the plate, cover tightly and boil. Steamed Salmon with Black Beans (page 61) is one example of this moist-cooking method. Salmon steaks are seasoned with a zesty marinade, steamed and sprinkled with a touch of peanut oil, bringing out the best in the ingredients without making the fish oily.

And plan on serving Chinese Jellied Seafood Mold (page 69) at your next buffet. Fresh shellfish and vegetables are enveloped in a delicately seasoned aspic, the perfect partner for spicier foods. With the dish conveniently prepared ahead, all you'll need to do at serving time is wait for the compliments!

Fish

Tuna Egg Fu Yung

4 servings

4 eggs
1 6½-ounce can tuna, rinsed, drained and flaked
1 cup bean sprouts, rinsed and drained
¼ cup chopped water chestnuts
3 green onions (white part only), chopped

3 tablespoons finely chopped celery
2 tablespoons slivered almonds
  Soy sauce
  Salt and freshly ground pepper
2 to 3 tablespoons peanut oil
  Freshly steamed rice

Beat eggs to blend in medium bowl. Add tuna, bean sprouts, water chestnuts, green onion and celery and mix well. Blend in almonds. Season with soy sauce, salt and pepper. Heat 2 tablespoons oil in heavy skillet over medium heat. Drop mixture into skillet by heaping tablespoon, patting gently to flatten. Fry until golden, turning once and adding more oil to skillet if necessary. Serve with rice and additional soy sauce.

Grilled Tuna with Sauce of Soy and Rice Vinegar

A zesty East/West entrée.

4 servings

2 teaspoons wasabi (Japanese green horseradish powder)
1 tablespoon (about) water

2 pounds skinned fresh tuna fillets (¼ inch thick)
⅓ cup oriental sesame oil

½ cup low-salt soy sauce
¼ cup rice vinegar

½ cup (1 stick) unsalted butter, room temperature
3 tablespoons snipped fresh chives

  Small spinach leaves
8 slices pickled ginger
4 cooked crayfish

Combine wasabi with enough water to make thick paste. Cover and set aside.
    Prepare barbecue. Brush tuna with sesame oil. Grill for 1½ minutes on each side (fish fillets will be just pink inside) or to desired doneness.
    Meanwhile, bring soy sauce and vinegar to simmer in small saucepan. Remove from heat and whisk in butter 1 tablespoon at a time. Mix in chives.
    Cover plates with spinach and top with tuna. Arrange ginger and dab of wasabi on fish. Spoon sauce around fish. Garnish with crayfish and serve.

Japanese Miso-grilled Fish Steaks

This classic marinade works best with oily fish such as mackerel or snapper.

4 to 6 servings

½ cup miso
6 tablespoons water
¼ cup mirin (syrupy rice wine)
4 to 6 ½- to ¾-inch-thick fish slices or steaks, patted dry

1 tablespoon toasted sesame seeds
4 watercress or parsley sprigs

Mix miso, water and wine in heavy small saucepan and cook over low heat until mixture forms thick paste, stirring occasionally, about 4 minutes.

Pour mixture into flat dish. Arrange fish on top in single layer. Let stand 10 minutes. Turn fish over. Cover and refrigerate at least 6 hours, or overnight.

Prepare charcoal grill or preheat broiler. Drain fish, reserving marinade for another use. Grill fish 2 inches from heat source until opaque, about 3 minutes per side. Arrange on platter. Sprinkle with sesame seeds. Garnish with watercress or parsley sprigs and serve.

Steamed Salmon with Black Beans

Adding fresh banana chilies to the marinade will make this dish spicy-hot.

4 servings

2 tablespoons light soy sauce
1 to 2 tablespoons dry Sherry
1 teaspoon oriental sesame oil
1/4 teaspoon salt (or more to taste)
1/4 teaspoon freshly ground pepper
1/4 teaspoon sugar
1 tablespoon salted black beans, rinsed, drained and squeezed dry with fingertips
1/2 teaspoon chopped fresh ginger

2 to 3 salmon steaks of equal thickness (about 1 3/4 pounds total)

2 green onions, cut into 2-inch slivers
3 tablespoons peanut oil

Combine soy sauce, Sherry, sesame oil, salt, pepper and sugar in measuring cup and mix well. Mince beans very finely with ginger. Arrange fish on flameproof plate. Rub bean mixture over both sides of fish. Pour soy sauce mixture over. Marinate 2 hours.

Bring water to rapid boil in steamer (preferably Chinese). Set plate with fish in steamer. Cover and steam until fish tests done, about 9 minutes for every inch of thickness.

Transfer fish to serving dish. Sprinkle with green onion. Warm small saucepan over medium heat. Add oil and heat until it just begins to smoke. Drizzle over fish. Serve immediately.

Sweet Vinegared Fish

This is an easy method of cooking whole fish. The tangy vinegar sauce is a perfect complement.

2 main-course servings or 4 servings as part of multi-course Chinese meal

1 2-pound fresh whole rock cod or red snapper
1 teaspoon salt
2 1/2 tablespoons cornstarch

7 tablespoons water
1 1/2 tablespoons dark soy sauce
1 tablespoon (scant) rice vinegar
1 teaspoon sugar
1/8 teaspoon Chinese rice wine or dry white wine

2 tablespoons chopped green onion
1 tablespoon minced garlic
1 tablespoon minced fresh ginger

1/4 cup vegetable oil

Lemon slices
4 cilantro sprigs
Sliced green onion (green part only)

Pat fish dry with paper towels. Using sharp knife, cut fish to the bone in 3 places on each side. Rub salt over outside of fish; repeat with cornstarch.

Mix water, soy sauce, vinegar, sugar and wine in small bowl. Combine 2 tablespoons green onion, garlic and ginger in another bowl.

Heat wok over high heat. Add oil and heat 30 seconds. Reduce heat to medium-high. Slide fish down side of wok into oil and fry until golden brown, gently turning once with 2 spatulas, about 2 minutes on each side. (If fish sticks, reduce heat slightly.) Add soy and green onion mixtures. Cover and cook 4 minutes. Turn fish over, using 2 spatulas. Increase heat to high, cover and cook until fish just turns opaque, about 4 minutes. (If fish sticks, reduce heat and add 1 teaspoon water.)

Transfer fish to platter. Pour sauce over. Garnish with lemon slices, parsley and green onion and serve.

Coral Fish Slices

2 main-course servings or 4 servings as part of multi-course Chinese meal

10 ounces skinned and boned fresh red snapper or rock cod fillets
1 egg white
2 tablespoons plus ½ teaspoon cornstarch
1 teaspoon salt
¼ teaspoon freshly ground white pepper

5 small tomatoes (14 ounces), peeled, halved and seeded

Oil for deep frying
1 tablespoon minced garlic
1 tablespoon minced fresh ginger
¾ tablespoon minced green onion (green part only)

Cut fish into 1 × ½ × ½-inch pieces. Combine in small bowl with egg white, cornstarch, ½ teaspoon salt and ¼ teaspoon pepper. Marinate for 1 to 3 hours in refrigerator.

Drain tomatoes on paper towels 15 minutes. Cut into ½-inch chunks.

Heat oil in wok or heavy large saucepan to 350°F. Add fish and fry until outer layer is crusty, about 1¼ minutes. Remove using slotted spoon. Pour out all but 2 tablespoons oil from wok. Heat over high heat 1 minute. Add garlic and ginger and sauté 30 seconds. Add tomato and ½ teaspoon salt. Cook 45 seconds, mashing with spatula. Add fish and stir 10 seconds. Transfer to platter. Garnish with green onion. Serve immediately.

Trout Shioyaki with Mint, Garlic and Soy

Shioyaki is the incomparable Japanese method of salt-broiling fish. To cook as the Japanese do so that the fish appears to be swimming when served, insert a skewer where the head meets the body, then out throught the base of the tail.

4 servings

4 ¾- to 1-pound trout or other fresh fish
Sea salt
2 to 3 tablespoons minced fresh mint *or* coriander

2 tablespoons soy sauce
2 large garlic cloves, minced
Lemon wedges

To prepare a whole fish, dip the tail and fins into salt, then wrap them in foil to prevent burning. Salt the rest of the fish *lightly* and let stand for 30 minutes.

Prepare charcoal grill. Combine mint, soy and garlic and rub evenly over fish. Grill until fish just loses its translucency. Serve with lemon.

Thai Fish Quenelles and Vegetable Curry (Gaeng Look Cheen Pla)

The freshly ground spices add a subtle but essential flavor and texture.

6 servings

Spice Paste
5 dried red chilies, chopped, or
  1 teaspoon cayenne pepper
1½ tablespoons coriander seeds
  1 teaspoon cumin seeds
  ½ teaspoon black peppercorns
  5 medium shallots, minced
  5 medium garlic cloves, minced
  4 cilantro sprigs, minced
  1 lemongrass stalk, minced, *or* peel of 1 lemon (yellow part only), finely minced
1½ teaspoons dried powdered galangal (Siamese ginger) or 1 teaspoon powdered ginger
  ½ teaspoon shrimp paste (kapee) or anchovy paste

Quenelles
12 ounces fish fillets, coarsely chopped

  ½ teaspoon cornstarch
  ¼ teaspoon salt
  ¼ teaspoon freshly ground pepper
  1 quart cold salted water

  3 tablespoons vegetable oil
  2 cups thin coconut milk *or* 2 cups lowfat milk flavored with ½ teaspoon coconut extract
  2 cups white cabbage, cut into 2-inch squares (5 ounces)
  2 tablespoons fish sauce (nam pla)
  2 cups thick coconut milk *or* 2 cups whole milk flavored with 1 teaspoon coconut extract
  1 cup green beans, cut diagonally into 2-inch pieces and blanched until crisp-tender (4 ounces trimmed)

For spice paste: Combine chilies, coriander seeds, cumin and peppercorns in large mortar and crush to powder. Transfer to processor if desired. Add shallot, garlic, cilantro, lemongrass, ginger and shrimp paste and mix until smooth. Set aside.

For quenelles: Place fish fillets in mortar, food processor or blender and pulverize to fine paste. Mix in cornstarch, salt and pepper. Shape into 1-inch balls. Gently transfer to bowl of cold salted water. Set aside until ready to use. (*Quenelles can be prepared 1 day ahead. Refrigerate stored in cold salted water or place in airtight bags and freeze.*)

Heat oil in wok over high heat. Add spice paste and stir-fry until mixture darkens and aroma mellows. Blend in thin coconut milk and bring to boil, stirring occasionally. Add cabbage and boil until tender, about 5 minutes. Drain quenelles; add to wok. Return liquid to boil and cook until quenelles rise to surface. Reduce heat and simmer 2 minutes. Cook, stirring constantly, 2 minutes. Add beans and cook 1 minute. Transfer to dish and serve.

Crisp Whole Fish with Gingered Vegetable Sauce

The garnish can be prepared several hours ahead and kept crisp in a bowl of ice water in the refrigerator. All ingredients should be readied ahead and kept in separate dishes.

6 servings

1 3- to 3-1/2 pound rock cod, sea bass, carp, yellowtail or red snapper, cleaned
1/4 to 1/2 cup cornstarch

Oil for deep frying

Sauce
1 1/2 tablespoons dark soy sauce
1 tablespoon rice vinegar
1 teaspoon dry Sherry
1 teaspoon sugar
1/2 cup water

3 tablespoons vegetable oil
1 red bell pepper, seeded and cut into julienne
1 green bell pepper, seeded and cut into julienne
1 1/2 tablespoons slivered fresh ginger
2 tablespoons minced green onion

1 carrot, cut into fine 2-inch-long julienne
2 green onions, cut into fine 2-inch-long julienne

Slash fish horizontally all the way to bone at 1-inch intervals. Hold fish up by tail and sprinkle cornstarch into slashes and over fish.

Pour enough oil into wok or deep fryer to come within 2 inches of top. Heat to 400°F. Add fish and fry until cooked through, turning occasionally, about 20 minutes. Set aside; keep warm.

For sauce: Combine first 5 ingredients in small bowl. Heat oil in heavy medium skillet over high heat. Add bell peppers and stir until just beginning to soften, about 2 minutes. Add ginger and minced green onion and stir until aromatic, about 30 seconds. Add liquid ingredients and bring to boil, scraping up any browned bits.

Pour sauce over fish. Garnish with carrot and green onions. Serve immediately.

Steamed Sablefish with Ginger and Szechwan Peppercorn Sauce

6 servings

3 cups (6 sticks) well-chilled butter
4 medium shallots, chopped
4 cups dry saké
1/2 cup fresh lemon juice
1/4 cup Szechwan peppercorns, lightly roasted
2 2-inch pieces ginger, peeled and chopped

4 cups fish stock, preferably homemade
2 cups whipping cream

6 8-ounce sablefish fillets (rockfish or ling cod may be substituted)
Sautéed spinach

Melt 2 tablespoons butter in heavy large saucepan over medium-low heat. Add shallots and stir until translucent, about 5 minutes. Add saké, lemon juice, peppercorns and ginger. Increase heat to high and cook until reduced by half. Add fish stock and cook until reduced to 1 1/2 cups. Add cream and cook until reduced to 1 1/2 cups. Remove from heat and whisk in 3 tablespoons butter. Place over low heat and whisk in remaining butter 1 tablespoon at a time, incorporating each piece completely before adding next. Strain sauce into another saucepan. Keep warm in water bath.

Steam fish until opaque, about 9 minutes per 1-inch thickness. Arrange bed of sautéed spinach on each plate. Top with fish. Spoon some of sauce over each and serve.

 *Shellfish*

Scrambled Eggs with Crabmeat (Dadar Kepiting)

Watercress is the traditional garnish for this delicate Indonesian brunch dish.

6 servings

4 eggs
1 cup coarsely flaked crabmeat
2 medium-size green onions, thinly sliced
¼ teaspoon freshly ground white pepper

Salt
1 tablespoon corn oil
Watercress sprigs

Beat eggs to blend in medium bowl. Mix in crabmeat, onions, pepper and salt. Heat oil in heavy large skillet over medium-low heat. Add egg mixture and whisk slowly until cooked to desired doneness. Turn out onto platter. Garnish with watercress and serve.

Stir-fried Lobster with Ginger and Green Onions

2 main-course servings or 4 servings as part of multi-course meal

2 cups vegetable oil (for frying)
1 1¼-pound uncooked lobster, cut into 14 pieces

⅔ cup finely shredded green onions (white part only)
2 to 3 tablespoons 2-inch-long julienne of peeled fresh ginger
½ teaspoon minced garlic

¼ cup Kung Bao Sauce (see page 66)
1 tablespoon Cornstarch Mixture (see page 66)
1 tablespoon Chinese rice wine or dry Sherry
1 tablespoon oriental sesame oil
Additional shredded green onion

Heat vegetable oil in wok or deep saucepan over medium-high heat until bubbles form around dry wooden chopstick inserted in oil (about 350°F). Increase heat to high. Add lobster and cook until shells turn bright red, about 45 to 60 seconds. Carefully pour mixture into colander set over stainless steel bowl.

Return 2 tablespoons vegetable oil to wok or heavy large skillet over high heat. Add ⅔ cup green onions, ginger and garlic. Stir-fry until aromatic, 20 to 30 seconds. Mix in lobster, kung bao sauce and cornstarch mixture. Stir in wine and sesame oil. Transfer to warm platter. Garnish with additional green onion and serve immediately.

Stir-fried Mussels with Kung Bao Sauce

4 servings

20 large mussels, scrubbed
½ cup cold water

3 tablespoons vegetable oil
6 green onions, white part cut into julienne, green part cut into 2-inch lengths
1 small serrano or other hot green chili, seeded and minced
1 tablespoon minced fresh ginger

1 tablespoon minced cilantro
1 teaspoon minced garlic
⅓ cup Kung Bao Sauce*
2 tablespoons Cornstarch Mixture**
1 tablespoon Chinese rice wine or dry Sherry
1 tablespoon oriental sesame oil

Combine mussels and water in wok or large saucepan. Cover and boil until mussels begin to open, 3 to 4 minutes. Transfer opened mussels to colander, using slotted spoon. Cook remaining mussels 5 minutes more; discard any that do not open. (*Can be prepared 8 hours ahead and refrigerated. Bring to room temperature before continuing.*)

Heat wok or heavy large skillet over high heat. Add oil, then green onions, chili, ginger, cilantro and garlic. Stir-fry until aromatic, about 30 seconds. Add mussels, kung bao sauce and cornstarch mixture. Stir until sauce thickens and mussels are heated through, about 1 minute. Mix in rice wine and sesame oil and serve immediately.

*Kung Bao Sauce

Makes about ¾ cup

¼ cup chicken stock
6 to 8 ¼-inch slices green onion tops
3 1 × ⅛-inch slivers fresh ginger
1 tablespoon dark soy sauce
1 tablespoon light soy sauce
1½ teaspoons cornstarch

1 teaspoon Chinese rice wine or dry Sherry
1 teaspoon distilled white vinegar
1 teaspoon Chinese red vinegar or distilled white vinegar
½ teaspoon sugar
Pinch of white pepper

Mix all ingredients in bowl. (*Can be stored 1 week in refrigerator.*)

**Cornstarch Mixture

Make a batch of this mixture before starting to cook a Chinese meal; use it to thicken all the sauces.

Makes about 1 cup

1 cup warm water
¼ cup cornstarch

Mix water and cornstarch in bowl. Stir thoroughly with fork before using.

Seven Steps to the Perfect Chinese Stir-fry

Stir-frying is one of the most frequently used Chinese cooking methods, and it may be the ultimate technique for busy cooks. Use vegetables on hand, perhaps add a little leftover meat or seafood, and you will have a complete meal-in-one. And remember that in stir-frying all the seasoning is done in the kitchen by the cook; don't drown everything in soy sauce at the dining table.

- All pieces of each ingredient should be as uniform as possible in shape and size.
- If food is cut into small pieces it will cook more quickly and will retain its fresh natural flavor and texture.
- Never cook more than one pound of meat or shellfish at a time or it will end up boiling in its own juices.
- All stir-frying should be done over the highest possible heat.
- Read the recipe instructions carefully before you begin and line the ingredients up on the counter in the order they are to be added to the wok; the most dense ingredients will go in first, the least dense last.
- Undercook everything—the wok is very hot and the degree of doneness of ingredients can be deceptive.
- Serve the finished dish *immediately*.

Stir-fried Shrimp Sampan Style

2 to 3 servings

8 ounces uncooked medium shrimp
2 tablespoons peanut oil or vegetable oil
2 garlic cloves, coarsely chopped
1 teaspoon finely chopped dried red chilies
1/4 teaspoon freshly ground pepper
Soy sauce

Using scissors, cut along back of each shrimp shell to devein, but do not remove shell. Pat shrimp dry with paper towel. Heat oil in wok or large skillet over medium-high heat. When oil is very hot (almost to smoking point), add shrimp, garlic and peppers and stir-fry until shrimp are uniformly pink and cooked through, about 4 minutes. Transfer to heated platter and serve immediately with soy sauce.

Thai Garlic Shrimp (Gung Kratiem)

4 servings

Roots (if possible) and 1 inch stems from 2 bunches cilantro
1 large garlic head, cloves separated
1/4 cup vegetable oil
1/2 teaspoon freshly ground pepper
1 pound large shrimp, peeled and deveined
1 cup water
3 to 3 1/2 tablespoons fish sauce (nam pla)
2 tablespoons sugar
Sliced cucumbers, radishes and tomatoes (optional garnishes)
Freshly cooked rice

Finely mince cilantro and garlic in processor using on/off turns, or mash in mortar with pestle until smooth paste forms.

Heat oil in wok or heavy large skillet over medium-high heat. Add garlic mixture and pepper and stir until garlic is golden brown. Add shrimp and stir to coat with oil. Add water, fish sauce and sugar and bring to boil. Transfer to platter. Garnish with sliced vegetables if desired. Serve immediately with rice.

Kaye's Stir-fried Shrimp and Vegetables

4 servings

2 tablespoons vegetable oil
3 medium-size green onions, sliced on diagonal into ½-inch pieces
1 medium carrot, thinly sliced on diagonal
1 medium celery stalk, sliced into ¼-inch pieces
½ medium crookneck squash, thinly sliced
1 tomato, chopped
4 strips crisply cooked bacon, crumbled

2 to 3 tablespoons coarsely chopped cilantro
1 tablespoon Thai seafood sauce or oriental chili paste with garlic
1 teaspoon red Thai curry paste or oriental curry paste
12 jumbo shrimp, peeled and deveined
Freshly cooked rice

Heat oil in large cast-iron skillet over high heat. Stir-fry green onions, carrot and celery until onions are browned, 2 to 3 minutes. Add squash, tomato and bacon. Reduce heat to medium and stir in cilantro, seafood sauce and curry paste. Add shrimp and stir-fry just until pink. Serve hot over rice.

Philippine Prawns with Green Beans and Coconut

The bright pink of the prawns is a beautiful contrast to the green beans.

12 servings

1 16-ounce package frozen unsweetened coconut milk, thawed
2 medium garlic cloves, pounded to paste in mortar with pestle
2 pound Chinese or regular green beans, trimmed and cut into 2-inch pieces

2 pounds jumbo shrimp or prawns, unpeeled, cut down back and deveined
½ teaspoon salt

Bring coconut milk and garlic to simmer in wok or heavy large skillet over medium heat. Stir until mixture thickens to consistency of whipping cream, about 7 minutes. Add green beans, cover and simmer 6 minutes, stirring occasionally. Mix in shrimp and salt. Cover and simmer until shrimp just turn opaque, about 15 minutes (sauce will curdle slightly). Transfer to platter and serve immediately.

Shrimp Steamed in Beer with Oriental Dressing

The sesame-enchanced dressing adds a pleasant nuance to the shrimp.

8 servings

2 12-ounce cans beer
3 tablespoons fresh lemon juice
2 tablespoons minced fresh parsley
2 garlic cloves
1 bay leaf
1 teaspoon minced fresh thyme
1 teaspoon celery seed
1/8 teaspoon ground red pepper
2 1/2 pounds large shrimp, unshelled

Oriental Dressing
1/2 cup rice vinegar (unseasoned)

1 tablespoon Dijon mustard
1 teaspoon fresh lemon juice
1 1/2 cups vegetable oil
1/4 teaspoon oriental sesame oil
Salt and freshly ground pepper

Green onion brushes tied in center with blanched chive
Lemon slices, halved
Croûtes

Bring first 8 ingredients to boil in medium saucepan. Add shrimp, adjust heat so water is barely simmering and cook until just pink, about 3 minutes. Drain. Peel and devein shrimp; cool. Refrigerate about 2 hours.

For dressing: Blend vinegar, mustard and juice in small bowl. Whisk in oils in thin stream. Season with salt and pepper. (*Can be made 1 day ahead and refrigerated.*) Stir half of dressing into shrimp and chill 30 minutes.

Arrange shrimp on plates and garnish with green onion brushes and lemon slices. Serve with Croûtes, passing remaining dressing separately.

*Croûtes

Makes about 30

1/2 cup olive oil
1/2 cup clarified butter
1 loaf French bread, cut into 1/2-inch-thick slices

Salt and freshly ground pepper

Preheat oven to 300°F. Combine oil and butter in small bowl. Dip both sides of bread slices in mixture and arrange on baking sheet. Sprinkle with salt and pepper. Bake until golden brown, about 25 minutes. Serve warm or at room temperature. (*Can be prepared 1 day ahead. Cool; wrap airtight. Rewarm in 300°F oven about 5 minutes.*)

Chinese Jellied Seafood Mold

10 buffet servings

1 pound bay scallops
13 ounces small shrimp, shelled and deveined
1/2 cup shelled fresh peas

2 cups clarified chicken stock, degreased
2 tablespoons light soy sauce
2 tablespoons dry Sherry
1/2 teaspoon sugar

Juice of one 1-inch piece fresh ginger
Salt and freshly ground white pepper
1 envelope unflavored gelatin
1/4 cup thinly sliced green onion
1/4 cup chopped celery leaves
1 cup cooked king crab claw meat, cut into 1/2-inch cubes

Cook scallops and shrimp separately in gently simmering water until just opaque. Drain well. Cook peas in boiling water until tender; drain.

Bring stock, soy sauce, Sherry, sugar, ginger juice, salt and pepper to simmer in medium saucepan over medium-high heat. Remove from heat. Add gelatin and stir to dissolve completely. Sprinkle bottom of shallow 1½-quart mold (such as 11-inch pie plate) with green onion and celery leaves. Arrange scallops, shrimp, peas and crabmeat over top. Pour in broth. Refrigerate until set. Unmold onto large platter and serve immediately.

Chinese Tofu Casserole

4 servings as part of multi-course Chinese meal

1 4 × 2-inch square tofu

Marinade for tofu
½ small onion, grated
1 ½-inch piece fresh ginger, grated
2 tablespoons mirin (syrupy rice wine) or dry Sherry
2 tablespoons dark soy sauce
1 tablespoon light soy sauce
1 teaspoon sugar
1 teaspoon oriental sesame oil

Marinade for shrimp
2 tablespoons mirin or Sherry
1 tablespoon cornstarch
½ teaspoon coarse salt or
¼ teaspoon regular salt
8 large shrimp, peeled, deveined and halved lengthwise

Peanut oil for deep frying

Batter
2 small eggs
2 tablespoons ice-cold club soda
2 tablespoons all purpose flour
1 tablespoon cornstarch

3 tablespoons peanut oil
1 cup chicken stock
12 snow peas, sliced diagonally into ⅛-inch pieces

2 cups shredded Chinese cabbage
¼ cup water
1 tablespoon cornstarch
¼ teaspoon hot chili paste with garlic or hot pepper sauce
Cilantro sprigs
Freshly cooked rice

If using Chinese tofu, cut off firm outside layer. Cut Chinese tofu in half horizontally (Japanese is thinner and may be left whole). Wrap pieces in cheesecloth and press with weight, changing cloth as necessary until all excess moisture is squeezed out (this may take 1½ hours). Using sharp knife, cut tofu into 1 × ½-inch pieces.

For tofu marinade: Combine all ingredients for tofu marinade on large plate. Add cut tofu and marinate 1 hour, turning after 30 minutes.

For shrimp marinade: Combine mirin, cornstarch and salt. Add shrimp, cover and refrigerate about 1 hour, stirring several times.

Preheat oil to 360°F. Mix ingredients for batter just before using. Dip tofu into batter and deep fry in small batches until pieces are brown and float to surface. Remove with chopsticks or slotted spoon and drain well on paper towels.

Heat 3 tablespoons oil in wok. Add shrimp and stir-fry 1 minute. Add tofu, chicken stock and snow peas; stir, then cover and simmer 3 minutes.

Turn cabbage into serving dish. Remove cover from wok. Combine water, cornstarch, and chili paste. Add to wok and cook briefly until sauce is clear and thickened. Spoon over cabbage and garnish with cilantro. Serve immediately with freshly cooked rice.

6 ❦ Poultry

It's adaptable, nourishing, thrifty, readily available—and delicious. No wonder, then, that poultry features prominently in virtually every one of the world's cuisines. And in the Orient, where space for raising larger livestock is at a premium, cooks have devised a truly sensational array of poultry dishes.

From Shanghai, which boasts one of China's most vibrant regional cuisines, comes Red-in-Snow with White Chicken (page 80)—an easy stir-fry using a typical Chinese vegetable that is available canned in most oriental markets. Also Shanghainese is Chinese Onion Duck (page 81), in which the bird is braised in a savory sauce. The crisp textures and fresh flavors of Cantonese cooking appear in Lemon Chicken (page 75), while General Tso's Chicken (page 75) and Stir-fried Chicken with Chilies and Peanuts (page 74) represent Szechwan food at its fiery best.

Other Asian lands offer altogether different specialties. Flavored with soy sauce, saké and ginger, Japanese Double-fried Chicken with Ginger and Sesame Oil (page 80) is Japan's answer to our own Southern fried chicken—and like its American counterpart, this Japanese favorite makes perfect picnic fare when served cold. Another unusual twist on an American standby is Indonesia's Spicy Chicken Croquettes (page 74), flavored with an intriguing blend of coriander, cumin and garlic.

Indonesian cuisine also features some of the world's most delicious recipes for duck, of which a trio is included here. Twice-cooked Duck Bali Style (page 82) is stuffed with spinach and perfumed with a whole spice rack of seasonings. Hot, garlicky Duck in Macadamia Sauce (page 83), a great party or buffet dish, is completely do-ahead; Grilled Duck in Coconut Milk (page 83) is yet another mix of rich and unusual flavors.

In addition to these fried, braised and grilled dishes, the chapter is rounded out with a medley of cool East/West-style chicken salads and with a versatile poultry stuffing made of brown rice and sweet Chinese sausage. And all this variety is just a sampling of the fabulous poultry dishes that oriental cooking has to offer.

Chicken Slices with Szechwan Sesame Sauce

A simple do-ahead entrée, the chicken can be poached two days before serving, and the sauce will keep for eight hours. Refrigerate both until ready to use.

2 servings

1 whole chicken breast

  Romaine or spinach leaves
2 garlic cloves, minced
3 tablespoons tahini or peanut butter
2 to 3 tablespoons chili oil
2 tablespoons minced fresh ginger

2 tablespoons light soy sauce
2 tablespoons oriental sesame oil
2 teaspoons sugar
1½ teaspoons rice vinegar
¼ teaspoon ground Szechwan peppercorns
  Cilantro or parsley sprigs

Simmer chicken in water to cover until firm to touch and no pink shows close to bone, about 10 minutes. Remove from water and cool. Skin and bone chicken; separate halves. Cut each half diagonally into thin slices.

Mound romaine on 2 plates. Top with chicken. Blend remaining ingredients except cilantro in small bowl. Spoon sauce over chicken. Garnish with cilantro or parsley and serve.

Cantonese Chicken Salad

A tangy and crunchy salad.

6 to 8 servings

2 medium heads iceberg lettuce, shredded
1 cup chopped celery
¼ cup chopped cilantro
1¾ cups chow mein noodles
¼ cup vegetable oil
1¾ pounds boned chicken breasts, skinned and sliced into 2-inch strips

12 ounces sliced water chestnuts, drained
1¾ cups snow peas, each cut diagonally into 3 pieces
2¾ cups Curry Dressing*
¼ cup sliced almonds
10 radishes, thinly sliced
2 medium-size green onions, finely chopped

Combine lettuce, celery and cilantro in glass salad bowl. Spread noodles over. Heat oil in heavy large skillet over medium-high heat. Add chicken and stir until lightly browned, about 2 minutes. Add water chestnuts and snow peas and stir 1 minute. Remove mixture using slotted spoon and arrange over salad. Add 2 cups of dressing and toss well. Garnish with almonds, radishes and green onions and serve. Pass remaining dressing separately.

*Curry Dressing

Makes 2¾ cups

3 tablespoons dry white wine
2 tablespoons unsweetened pineapple juice
2 tablespoons fresh lemon juice
2 tablespons firmly packed light brown sugar

1½ tablespoons curry powder
2 teaspoons soy sauce
1 teaspoon onion powder
  Pinch of garlic powder
2 cups mayonnaise

Combine all ingredients except mayonnaise in nonaluminum bowl and stir until brown sugar dissolves. Add mayonnaise and blend until dressing is smooth.

Chinese Chicken Salad

8 main-course servings

Dressing
- ¼ cup vegetable oil
- 3 tablespoons rice vinegar
- 2 tablespoons sugar
- 1 tablespoon oriental sesame oil
- 2 teaspoons soy sauce
- 1½ teaspoons dry mustard
- ½ teaspoon grated fresh ginger

- 3 whole chicken breasts, cooked and shredded

- 1 head Chinese cabbage (about 2 pounds), shredded
- 1 16½-ounce jar roasted unsalted peanuts
- 5 medium-size green onions, thinly sliced
- 3 ounces rice stick noodles (mai fun), cooked according to package instructions

For dressing: Combine all ingredients in jar and shake well.

Mix chicken, cabbage, peanuts and green onions in large bowl. Pour dressing over and toss gently. Add noodles and toss again. Serve chilled.

Roasted Chicken Slivers Seasoned with Sesame Oil

Creative lunch or brunch fare.

2 servings

Peanut Butter Dressing
- 2 tablespoons creamy peanut butter
- 2 tablespoons soy sauce
- 2 tablespoons rice vinegar
- 1 tablespoon Dijon mustard
- 1 tablespoon sugar
- 1 tablespoon grated fresh ginger
- ¾ teaspoon minced garlic
- ⅜ teaspoon oriental sesame oil
- ¼ teaspoon chili oil

- 2 chicken breasts (about 1 pound)
  Salt and freshly ground pepper

- 2 ounces rice stick noodles (mai fun)

- ½ carrot, peeled
- ½ celery stalk
- ½ leek
- ¼ fennel bulb, trimmed
- ⅓ cucumber, peeled and seeded
- 2 ounces enoki mushrooms, trimmed
- 2 green onions, minced

  Small spinach leaves, stems removed
  Red onion slices
  Green onions

For dressing: Mix first 9 ingredients in processor. (*Can be prepared 1 day ahead. Cover and store at room temperature.*)

Preheat oven to 400°F. Season chicken with salt and pepper. Place on baking pan and bake until just springy to touch, about 22 minutes. Cool.

Soak rice stick noodles in hot water to cover until softened, about 30 minutes.

Skin and bone chicken; cut into julienne. Place in large bowl. Cut carrot, celery, leek, fennel and cucumber into julienne. Add to chicken. Drain noodles well and cut into 2-inch pieces. Add to chicken. Mix in mushrooms and minced green onions.

Arrange spinach on plates. Top with chicken mixture. Garnish with red and green onions and serve, passing peanut butter dressing separately.

Chicken Teriyaki with Pineapple

4 servings

Marinade
- ³/₄ cup soy sauce
- ¹/₂ cup sugar
- ¹/₄ cup vegetable oil
- ¹/₄ cup saké
- 1 medium garlic clove, crushed
- ¹/₄ teaspoon ground ginger

- 1 pound boneless chicken breasts, skinned and cut into 1-inch cubes

- 8 large mushrooms
- 8 cherry tomatoes
- 1 large onion, cut into large chunks
- 1 large green bell pepper, seeded and cut into large chunks
- ¹/₄ fresh pineapple, peeled and cut into large chunks

For marinade: Combine all ingredients in large bowl and stir until sugar dissolves. Add chicken to marinade and refrigerate 45 minutes.

Prepare barbecue grill. Remove chicken from marinade, reserving marinade. Divide chicken pieces and remaining ingredients among four 12-inch skewers. Grill until chicken is browned, turning frequently and brushing with reserved marinade, about 10 minutes. Serve immediately.

Spicy Chicken Croquettes (Kroket Ayam)

The wonderful blend of flavors in this Indonesian dish is a reminder that the area was once known as the Spice Islands.

6 servings

- 1³/₄ pounds chicken breasts, boned, skinned and cut into pieces
- ¹/₄ cup thinly sliced green onion
- 1 teaspoon ground coriander
- ¹/₂ teaspoon salt or to taste
- ¹/₄ teaspoon ground cumin
- ¹/₄ teaspoon freshly ground pepper

- 1 medium garlic clove, minced
- 3 tablespoons all purpose flour or dry breadcrumbs
- 2 eggs, beaten to blend

Corn oil for frying
Lemon wedges (garnish)

Grind chicken to moderately smooth consistency in food processor. Mix in onion, coriander, salt, cumin, pepper and garlic. Divide mixture into 6 equal portions. Form each portion into egg shape; flatten to thickness of about 1 inch. Coat lightly with flour, dip into eggs, then coat with flour again, shaking off excess. (*Chicken croquettes can be prepared several hours ahead to this point, covered and refrigerated.*)

Pour oil into wok or heavy large skillet to depth of ¹/₂ inch and heat over medium heat. Add croquettes and fry until browned and lightly crisped, 3 to 4 minutes on each side. Remove from skillet and drain well on paper towels. Serve warm with lemon wedges.

Stir-fried Chicken with Chilies and Peanuts

3 to 4 servings

- 2 teaspoons soy sauce
- 1¹/₂ teaspoons cornstarch
- 1 garlic clove, minced
- 1 ¹/₂-inch piece fresh ginger, minced
- 2 whole chicken breasts, halved, skinned, boned and diced

- ¹/₄ cup peanut oil
- 1 cup skinned raw peanuts
- 4 dried red chilies

- 8 dried shiitake mushrooms, soaked in hot water 15 minutes, drained and thinly sliced
- 1 bunch green onions, sliced
- 1 teaspoon rice vinegar
- ¹/₂ teaspoon sugar
- 1 teaspoon oriental sesame oil
Freshly cooked rice

Combine soy sauce, cornstarch, garlic and ginger in medium bowl and mix well. Add chicken, tossing to coat evenly. Let stand at room temperature 15 minutes.

Heat oil in wok over high heat. Add peanuts and stir-fry until golden brown. Remove with slotted spoon and set aside. Add chilies and stir-fry until browned. Remove with slotted spoon and set aside. Add chicken and stir-fry 2 minutes. Blend in mushrooms, onion, vinegar and sugar and cook 1 minute. Return peanuts and chilies to wok, blending well. Add sesame oil and continue cooking 1 minute. Serve immediately over rice.

Lemon Chicken

4 servings

Marinade
  1 tablespoon vegetable oil
  2 teaspoons soy sauce
  1/2 teaspoon Sherry
    Pinch of freshly ground pepper
  4 unskinned chicken breast halves, boned and flattened to 1/2-inch thickness
    Cornstarch

Lemon Sauce
  3/4 cup water
  3 heaping tablespoons sugar
  2 tablespoons catsup
    Juice of 1 large lemon

  1 teaspoon vegetable oil
    Pinch of salt
  1 teaspoon cornstarch dissolved in small amount of water.

    Vegetable oil

  2/3 cup bean sprouts
  2/3 cup thinly sliced snow peas
  2/3 cup thinly sliced bamboo shoots
  1/2 cup thinly sliced water chestnuts
    Tomato wedges, lemon slices, green onion slices and crushed almonds

For marinade: Combine first 4 ingredients in small bowl. Rub over chicken, allowing excess to drain off. Coat lightly with cornstarch. Refrigerate at least 30 minutes.

For lemon sauce: Combine first 6 ingredients in small saucepan and bring to boil over medium-high heat, stirring occasionally. Add dissolved cornstarch and stir until slightly thickened. Keep warm.

Heat 1/2 inch of vegetable oil in large skillet over medium-high heat. Fry chicken until golden brown on both sides. Drain, then cut into strips 3/4 inch wide. Set aside and keep warm.

Wipe out skillet, add small amount of vegetable oil and heat over medium-high. Add bean sprouts, snow peas, bamboo shoots and water chestnuts and stir-fry until crisp-tender. Transfer to heated platter. Top with chicken and spoon lemon sauce over. Garnish with tomato wedges, lemon slices, green onions and almonds.

General Tso's Chicken

3 to 4 servings

  3 tablespoons soy sauce
  3 tablespoons rice vinegar
  3 tablespoons water
  1 large garlic clove, finely minced
  1 teaspoon finely minced fresh ginger
  4 whole chicken legs (including thigh), skinned and boned

  1 egg, beaten
  1 tablespoon cornstarch

  2 cups corn oil
  4 dried hot red chilies
  1/4 to 1/2 teaspoon dried red pepper flakes (optional)

Combine soy sauce, vinegar, water, garlic and ginger in small bowl; set aside. Cut each chicken leg into 6 pieces. Combine egg and cornstarch in large bowl and blend well. Add chicken pieces and toss to coat.

Heat oil in wok or deep fryer until very hot. Add chicken in batches and fry until crisp and browned on all sides, about 3 to 4 minutes. Drain on paper towel. Pour off all but 1 teaspoon oil from wok. Add chilies and red pepper flakes and toss over high heat several seconds. Return chicken to wok with soy sauce mixture and stir 2 minutes. Transfer to dish and serve immediately.

Chinese Chicken with Peanuts

4 servings

2 tablespoons peanut oil
1/3 cup raw peanuts, skinned and chopped
2 garlic cloves, pressed
2 green onions, chopped
1 dried medium chili pepper, chopped

2 whole chicken breasts, skinned and boned, cut into 1/2-inch strips
Snow peas (optional)
2 tablespoons soy sauce
2 tablespoons dry Sherry
Freshly cooked rice

Heat oil in wok or large skillet over high heat. Add peanuts, garlic, onion and chili pepper and stir-fry 1 minute. Push mixture to side of wok. Stir in chicken, adding more oil if necessary, and stir-fry until chicken is slightly browned, 2 to 3 minutes. Add snow peas if desired and stir-fry until crisp-tender, about 1 minute. Stir in soy sauce and Sherry and continue cooking about 1 minute. Serve over freshly cooked rice.

Chicken with Ginger Sauce

A zesty stir-fry from Chicago's Thai Room.

2 servings

1/3 cup dried black Chinese mushrooms
8 ounced boned chicken breast, skinned and cut into 3/4-inch cubes
Salt and freshly ground pepper
1 tablespoon water
2 teaspoons soy sauce
12 green onions

Vegetable oil for deep frying
3 tablespoons cornstarch

Sauce
2 cups chicken stock
1 1/2 tablespoons sugar

1 tablespoon soy sauce
1 tablespoon fish sauce (nam pla)
1 tablespoon oyster sauce
1 teaspoon distilled white vinegar
1/2 teaspoon salt
3 tablespoons cornstarch dissolved in 3 tablespoons cold water
1/3 cup finely slivered fresh ginger
1 green chili (such as Anaheim), thinly sliced
Freshly cooked rice

Soak mushrooms in hot water to cover until soft, about 30 minutes. Sprinkle chicken with salt and pepper. Mix water and soy sauce into chicken. Let stand 30 minutes. Thinly slice white part of green onions. Cut green parts into 1-inch-long sections.

Drain mushrooms and squeeze dry. Discard stems; thinly slice caps.

Heat oil in wok or heavy large skillet to 375°F. Toss chicken with 3 tablespoons cornstarch. Add to oil and cook until crisp and opaque, about 1 1/2 minutes. Drain on paper towels.

For sauce: Bring first 7 ingredients to boil in heavy large skillet. Reduce heat to medium-low. Stir through cornstarch mixture and add to sauce, blending until thickened and translucent, about 30 seconds. Mix in green onions, mushrooms, ginger, chili and chicken. Stir until hot, about 1 minute. Serve immediately with freshly cooked rice.

Homestyle Chicken

Use a cleaver to cut the chicken legs, or have your butcher do it.

4 servings

Marinated Chicken
2 tablespoons cornstarch
1 tablespoon beaten egg
1 tablespoon vegetable oil
1 teaspoon Chinese rice wine or dry Sherry
Pinch of freshly ground white pepper
4 medium chicken legs, cut into 3 pieces each, small ends discarded

2 cups vegetable oil (for frying)

Garlic-scented Spinach
2 tablespoons vegetable oil
1/4 teaspoon minced garlic
4 cups spinach leaves, stemmed
2 teaspoons chicken broth
Pinch of salt

3 to 4 medium garlic cloves, thinly sliced
6 1/4-inch-long pieces green onion tops
8 1/4-inch cubes peeled fresh ginger
1/3 cup Kung Bao Sauce (see page 66)
1 tablespoon Cornstarch Mixture (see page 66)
1 tablespoon Chinese rice wine or dry Sherry
1 tablespoon oriental sesame oil
1 teaspoon Chinese red vinegar or distilled white vinegar

For chicken: Mix first 5 ingredients in medium bowl. Add chicken and toss to coat (mixture will be dry). Refrigerate at least 2 hours or overnight.

Heat 2 cups oil in wok or deep saucepan over medium-high heat until bubbles form around dry wooden chopstick inserted in oil (about 350°F). Increase heat to high. Add chicken and stir to separate. Cook until no longer pink on outside and almost cooked through, about 2 minutes. Drain mixture in colander set over metal bowl. Clean and dry wok.

For spinach: Heat 1 tablespoon vegetable oil in wok or heavy large skillet over high heat. Add 1/4 teaspoon minced garlic, then spinach. Stir until coated with oil. Add broth and salt. Stir-fry just until spinach wilts, about 10 seconds. Transfer spinach to heated platter, using slotted spoon. Keep warm. Clean and dry wok.

Heat remaining 1 tablespoon oil in wok over high heat. Add sliced garlic, green onion and ginger. Toss 10 seconds. Add chicken, kung bao sauce and cornstarch mixture. Stir-fry until almost no liquid remains in bottom of wok, about 1 minute. Add rice wine, sesame oil and vinegar. Stir-fry to mix. Spoon over spinach and serve.

Oriental Chicken

4 servings

1 cup fresh orange juice
2 tablespoons dry Sherry
2 teaspoons soy sauce
2 whole chicken breasts, skinned, boned and halved

1/2 cup all purpose flour
1 egg
2 tablespoons (1/4 stick) butter
1 tablespoon vegetable oil
1 medium orange, sliced

Combine orange juice, Sherry and soy sauce in shallow glass dish. Add chicken and refrigerate overnight, turning once.

Place flour in shallow dish. Beat egg in another shallow dish. Remove chicken, reserving marinade. Dip chicken in flour, then in egg, and in flour again. Melt butter with oil in large skillet over medium heat. Add chicken and cook until browned and tender, 3 to 5 minutes on each side, depending on thickness. Remove chicken and keep warm. Add reserved marinade to skillet, scraping up any browned bits. Continue cooking until sauce thickens slightly, about 5 minutes. Arrange chicken on platter and pour sauce over. Garnish with orange slices and serve.

Chicken Lichee

6 to 8 servings

Sweet and Sour Sauce
1½ cups sugar
1 cup water
1 cup white vinegar
1 cup catsup
½ lemon, sliced, with slices quartered
3 ¼-inch slices fresh ginger, pressed
½ teaspoon salt

2 tablespoons peanut oil
2 pounds skinned and boned chicken breasts, cut into ½ × 2-inch strips

2 green peppers, seeded and cut into 1-inch squares
2 11-ounce cans whole peeled lichees, drained
¼ cup cornstarch dissolved in ¼ cup cold water
2 tablespoons sesame seeds, toasted (garnish)

For sauce: Combine first 7 ingredients in large saucepan and bring to boil, stirring frequently. Discard ginger. Reduce heat and keep sauce warm. (*Sweet and Sour Sauce can be frozen. Thaw and warm over medium-low heat before proceeding.*)

Heat wok or large saucepan over high heat several seconds. Add oil, swirling to coat sides. Quickly add chicken and stir-fry until meat just turns white. Remove pieces with slotted spoon and add to sauce. Add peppers and lichees to saucepan and bring to boil. Add dissolved cornstarch and continue cooking, stirring constantly, until thickened. Transfer to heated serving dish and garnish with toasted sesame seeds.

Sesame-crisped Chicken

4 servings

¼ cup soy sauce
2½ tablespoons dry Sherry
2 tablespoons vegetable oil
2 tablespoons orange marmalade
1 tablespoon honey
1 garlic clove, minced
1½ teaspoons oriental sesame oil

¼ teaspoon hot pepper sauce
2 chicken breasts, skinned and halved

6 3½-inch sesame breadsticks, crushed
2 tablespoons (¼ stick) butter

Combine first 8 ingredients in blender or food processor and mix well. Pour into shallow baking dish. Add chicken and turn several times to coat evenly. Cover and chill several hours or overnight, turning occasionally.

Preheat oven to 375°F. Grease 9 × 9-inch baking dish. Drain chicken, reserving marinade. Arrange in single layer in prepared dish. Sprinkle with crushed breadsticks and dot with butter. Bake, basting frequently with reserved marinade, until chicken is tender and juices run clear when pricked with fork, about 25 minutes. Serve hot.

Chinese Chicken in Lettuce Leaves

8 servings

¼ cup dry Sherry
¼ cup oyster sauce
2 tablespoons light soy sauce
1 teaspoon oriental sesame oil
½ teaspoon sugar
⅛ teaspoon cayenne pepper

3 large garlic cloves, peeled

½ pound (about 10) green onions, cut into thirds
2 large whole chicken breasts, boned, skinned, split, cut into pieces to fit feed tube, then frozen (slightly thawed but still firm)

4 cups peanut oil
⅓ cup walnut pieces

3 ounces rice sticks or bean thread noodles

1 3½-ounce can smoked oysters, drained and coarsely chopped
1 8-ounce can water chestnuts, drained and coarsely chopped
2 cups fresh bean sprouts *or* 1 7-ounce can, rinsed in cold water and thoroughly drained

16 to 24 large Boston lettuce leaves
Soy sauce

Combine first 6 ingredients in small mixing bowl and blend well.

In food processor, mince garlic by dropping through feed tube with machine running. Remove to bowl or piece of paper, scraping bowl and blade well.

Wedge onions vertically in feed tube and slice with medium slicer, using light pressure. Add to garlic. Insert chicken breasts vertically and slice with firm pressure. Remove and set aside.

Heat oil in wok or deep skillet to between 350°F and 375°F. Deep fry walnuts until crisp and light golden brown, 1 to 2 minutes. Remove and drain on paper towels.

Reheat oil to 375°F. If using noodles, separate as much as possible. Quickly deep fry rice sticks or noodles in small batches, submerging into oil with tongs; they should puff up immediately. *Do not brown.* Drain immediately on paper towels. Break into smaller serving pieces if necessary and mound in center of large serving platter. Remove all but 2 tablespoons oil from wok.

Chop nuts coarsely in food processor; remove and set aside.

Heat oil in wok until very hot. Add garlic and all but ¼ cup green onion and stir-fry briefly. Add chicken and stir-fry until opaque, pushing cooked pieces to sides of wok as they are done. (If using skillet, cook chicken in batches, removing as it is cooked.)

Add oysters and continue stir-frying with chicken 1 minute. Add water chestnuts 1 minute. Add water chestnuts, bean sprouts and reserved sauce and stir-fry only until heated through; *do not overcook.* Taste and adjust seasoning with additional soy sauce or salt, if needed. Mix in 3 tablespoons green onion.

Heap over noodles on serving platter and garnish with walnuts and remaining green onion. Arrange lettuce leaves around edge of platter. Serve immediately, letting each guest wrap a portion of noodles and chicken in lettuce leaf, and finish with a dash of soy sauce.

Red-in-Snow with White Chicken

Red-in-snow, a green leafy vegetable with red roots, adds an intriguing flavor to delicate chicken. It gets its name from the fact that it grows so early in the spring that the roots are often visible in the un-melted snow.

2 main-course servings or 4 servings as part of multi-course Chinese meal

9 ounces skinned and boned chicken breast
3 tablespoons vegetable oil
1 teaspoon cornstarch
½ teaspoon oriental sesame oil
¼ teaspoon salt
¼ teaspoon freshly ground white pepper

2 ounces canned red-in-snow (snow cabbage)
1 medium-size red bell pepper, seeded and cut into ¹⁄₁₀ × 1-inch strips
¼ teaspoon sugar

Cut chicken with the grain into ¹⁄₁₀ × ¹⁄₁₀ × 1-inch strips. Marinate with ½ tablespoon vegetable oil, cornstarch, sesame oil, salt and pepper 30 minutes at room temperature. (*Can be prepared 1 day ahead. Refrigerate.*)

Rinse red-in-snow under cold water 1 minute; drain. Chop finely.

Heat wok or heavy large skillet over high heat 1 minute. Add 1 tablespoon vegetable oil and heat 30 seconds. Add red-in-snow and bell pepper and stir 45 seconds. Mix in sugar. Remove mixture from wok. Wash wok and dry. Heat over high heat 1 minute. Add remaining 1½ tablespoons oil and heat almost white, about 1½ minutes. Return red-in-snow mixture to wok and toss 15 seconds. Transfer to platter and serve immediately.

Japanese Double-fried Chicken with Ginger and Sesame Oil (Kara-Age)

Because this is served at room temperature, it's perfect for picnics.

6 servings

1 2½- to 3-pound frying chicken
¼ cup Japanese soy sauce
¼ cup saké or dry Sherry
1 1-inch piece fresh ginger, minced
1 garlic clove, minced

½ cup all purpose flour
½ cup cornstarch

Salt
Kona sansho (Japanese fragrant pepper) or freshly ground pepper

Oil for deep frying
Oriental sesame oil
Lemon wedges

Cut chicken into 12 pieces, quartering breast and halving thighs crosswise. Combine soy sauce, saké, ginger and garlic in shallow baking dish. Add chicken, turning to coat all sides. Let chicken marinate at room temperature 30 minutes, turning frequently.

Combine flour, cornstarch, salt and kona sansho or pepper in shallow bowl. Dredge chicken in flour mixture, shaking off excess. Transfer chicken to waxed paper. Let stand until chicken is not completely white, about 10 minutes.

Heat oil in wok or deep fryer to 360°F, adding a few drops of sesame oil. Add chicken to oil in batches and fry just until lightly colored, about 45 seconds to 1 minute. Drain well on paper towels. Reduce oil temperature to 325°F. Return chicken to oil in batches and fry until coating is brown and chicken is cooked through, about 6 to 10 minutes. Drain on paper towels. Serve at room temperature with lemon wedges.

Spicy Glazed Chicken

8 servings

Marinade
- 2 large garlic cloves
- 1 1-inch slice fresh ginger, peeled
- 6 large green onions (3 ounces total), cut into 1-inch pieces
- Grated peel of 1 lemon
- 3 tablespoons hoisin sauce
- 3 tablespoons honey
- 3 tablespoons catsup
- 3 tablespoons soy sauce
- 2 tablespoons rice vinegar
- ½ teaspoon salt
- Freshly ground pepper

- 2 3-pound chickens, cut into serving pieces

For marinade: With machine running, drop garlic and ginger through processor feed tube and mince, stopping once to scrape down sides of bowl. Add green onion and lemon peel and blend well using on/off turns. Add all remaining ingredients except chicken and mix 5 seconds.

Pour equal amount of marinade into 2 large plastic storage bags. Transfer chicken pieces to bags and seal tightly. Let marinate at room temperature for 3 hours or refrigerate overnight (bring to room temperature before cooking).

Position rack in center of oven and preheat to 450°F. Line broiler pan or roasting pan with heavy-duty foil. Arrange chicken in pan in single layer, skin side down. Brush with marinade, coating well. Bake 20 minutes. Turn chicken over and baste generously with marinade. Continue baking until glazed and nicely browned, about 20 minutes. Baste chicken with any glaze remaining in bottom of pan, arrange on platter and serve immediately.

Chinese Onion Duck

Sweet simmered onions are a subtle counterpoint to this succulent duck.

4 servings

- 1 4-pound duck (preferably fresh)
- ⅔ cup water
- ¼ cup dark soy sauce
- 3 tablespoons sweet Sherry
- 2 heaping tablespoons rock sugar or brown sugar
- 1 teaspoon salt
- 2 pounds onions, cut into 1-inch chunks
- ¾ teaspoon cornstarch dissolved in 2 tablespoons cold water
- 6 cilantro sprigs (optional)

Discard fat from duck cavity. Pat duck dry. Place in heavy large saucepan. Add water, soy sauce, Sherry, sugar and salt and bring to boil. Reduce heat, cover and simmer about 1¾ hours, lifting duck frequently with wooden spoon inserted in cavity and turning every 30 minutes (duck should be tender when poked with chopstick around drumstick).

Transfer duck to platter breast side up. Tent with foil. Degrease cooking liquid. Add onions. Cook over high heat, stirring frequently, until onions are translucent, about 20 minutes.

Reduce heat to simmer. Blend cornstarch into onion mixture and sitr until thickened, about 3 minutes. Spoon over duck. Garnish with parsley if desired. Serve immediately.

Pressed Duck with Sweet and Sour Plum Sauce

8 to 10 appetizer servings

1 4- to 5-pound Long Island or
other domestic duckling, thawed
if frozen and cleaned
Boiling water
1 tablespoon five-spice powder
1 teaspoon salt

1 cup water chestnut powder
(see note)

Sweet and Sour Plum Sauce*

Oil for deep frying
Crushed toasted almonds or
macadamia nuts (garnish)

Place duck in large kettle or Dutch oven with enough boiling water to cover. Add spices and salt and simmer covered until tender, about 1 to 1¼ hours. Remove duck from liquid and let cool.

Remove meat from bones and discard skin. Pour chestnut powder into small baking pan (an 8-inch aluminum pan works well; powder should be ½ to ¾ inch deep). Press meat into powder. Cover and steam 30 minutes, or until powder has gelatinized into thick, heavy crust. Remove from steamer and let cool. Cover and chill until ready to complete.

About 30 minutes before serving time, prepare Sweet and Sour Plum Sauce; set aside and keep warm. Warm a serving platter in low oven.

Preheat oil in deep fryer to 375°F. Slice duck into bite-size chunks and fry quickly in batches until crisp and browned. Remove with slotted spoon and drain on paper towels. Repeat until cooking is completed. Serve immediately with Sweet and Sour Plum Sauce topped with nuts.

*Water chestnut powder is available in oriental markets and in some larger grocery stores. Do not substitute.

*Sweet and Sour Plum Sauce

Makes about 1½ cups

1 cup plum preserves or jam
½ cup water
2 tablespoons catsup

2 tablespoons cider vinegar
1 teaspoon cornstarch dissolved in
small amount of cold water

Combine first 4 ingredients in small saucepan and bring to boil. If sauce seems too thin, add cornstarch and water, stirring constantly until thickened. Reduce heat and keep warm until duck is prepared. Serve hot.

Twice-cooked Duck Bali Style (Bebek Betutu)

3 to 4 servings

2 tablespoons corn oil or
peanut oil
5 shallots, chopped
1 tablespoon firmly packed
brown sugar
1 teaspoon minced fresh ginger
1 teaspoon minced garlic
1 teaspoon ground coriander
1 teaspoon dried red pepper flakes
1 teaspoon salt
½ teaspoon freshly ground pepper
½ teaspoon turmeric
½ teaspoon ground cumin

½ teaspoon grated lemon peel
¼ teaspoon ground cloves
8 ounces spinach, stemmed

2 hard-cooked eggs, quartered
1 4½-pound duck
(loose fat discarded)

4 cups water
1 teaspoon salt
½ teaspoon turmeric

Heat oil over medium heat in heavy saucepan just large enough to accommodate duck. Add next 12 ingredients. Stir until aromatic, about 2 minutes. Add spinach and stir 1 minute. Cover and cook until wilted, about 2 minutes. Cool slightly.

Stir eggs into spinach stuffing. Fill duck with stuffing. Sew cavity closed.

Combine water, 1 teaspoon salt and ½ teaspoon turmeric in same saucepan. Add duck and bring to boil over medium heat. Cover saucepan and cook until duck begins to tenderize, turning once, about 45 minutes.

Preheat oven to 400°F. Transfer duck to roasting pan. Bake until brown and crisp, basting with ½ cup cooking liquid, 30 to 45 minutes. Cut duck into pieces. Serve immediately with stuffing.

Indonesian Duck in Macadamia Sauce (Bali Bebek)

Be sure to cook this dish one day ahead so the sauce can mellow.

6 servings

1 4½-pound duck (loose skin and fat discarded), cut into 8 pieces
⅓ cup lightly toasted macadamia nuts
½ cup sliced shallots
5 garlic cloves, sliced
2 tablespoons Kecap Manis (see page 13)

2 teaspoons dried red pepper flakes
2 teaspoons salt
1 teaspoon sugar
½ teaspoon turmeric
2 cups water
1 2-inch square lemon peel (yellow part only)
2 tablespoons fresh lemon juice

Discard any loose rib bones from ducks. Grind macadamia nuts to powder in processor. Add shallots, garlic, kecap manis, red pepper flakes, salt, sugar and turmeric. Process to smooth paste. Mix in water. Boil mixture in heavy large saucepan 5 minutes. Add duck, lemon peel and lemon juice. Reduce heat, cover and simmer 1 hour. Uncover pan, increase heat to medium and cook until duck is tender, turning occasionally, about 30 minutes. Cool. Cover and refrigerate duck overnight.

Discard fat from duck. Rewarm duck and sauce over medium heat. Transfer mixture to platter and serve immediately.

Indonesian Grilled Duck in Coconut Milk (Bebek Panggang Klaten)

Rice or rice noodles, a spicy sauce and a salad make good accompaniments.

3 to 4 servings

⅓ cup toasted macadamia nuts
3 cups canned coconut milk
1 small onion, sliced
4 garlic cloves, sliced
2 teaspoons ground coriander
2 teaspoons salt
1 teaspoon ground cumin
1 teaspoon sugar

½ teaspoon oriental or Indonesian shrimp paste (optional)

1 4- to 4½-pound duck, quartered, loose skin and fat discarded
1 4-inch square lemon peel (yellow part only)

Grind macadamia nuts to powder in processor. Add 1 cup coconut milk, onion, garlic, coriander, salt, cumin, sugar and shrimp sauce. Puree nut mixture to smooth paste.

Preheat broiler. Arrange duck skin side up in broiler pan. Cook 4 inches from heat until brown, about 5 minutes. Transfer to heavy large saucepan. Add nut mixture, remaining 2 cups coconut milk and lemon peel. Boil 2 minutes over medium heat, basting constantly. Reduce heat, cover and simmer until duck is tender, about 1½ hours. (*Can be prepared 1 day ahead. Let duck cool. Cover and refrigerate.*)

Preheat broiler. Discard fat from duck. Arrange duck skin side up in broiler pan. Cover with sauce. Cook 4 inches from heat until skin is crisp, about 6 minutes. Serve immediately.

Quail with Five-Flavor Marinade

8 first-course servings

2 ounces oriental rock sugar
(two 1-inch cubes)
2 tablespoons dark soy sauce
2 tablespoons Chinese rice wine or
dry Sherry
1 1-inch cube fresh ginger, peeled
and crushed

1 green onion
1 teaspoon five-spice powder
8 quail

4 cups vegetable oil (for frying)
Spice Dip*

Mix sugar, soy sauce, rice wine, ginger, green onion and five-spice powder in nonaluminum bowl. Add quail, turning to coat. Refrigerate at least 2 hours or overnight, turning occasionally.

Transfer quail and marinade to nonaluminum saucepan. Cover and bring to simmer. Remove mixture from heat. Let stand, covered, 30 minutes. Uncover and let quail cool in liquid.

Pat quail dry with paper towels. Halve lengthwise using poultry shears. Heat oil in wok until bubbles form around dry wooden chopstick inserted in oil (about 350°F). Fry quail in batches (do not crowd) until golden brown, turning once, about 2 minutes. Drain well on paper towels. Serve immediately and pass spice dip separately.

*Spice Dip

Makes about 2 tablespoons

4 teaspoons salt
2 teaspoons freshly ground pepper

½ teaspoon five-spice powder

Combine all ingredients in heavy small skillet over medium-high heat. Stir until aromatic, about 2 to 3 minutes.

Chinese Sausage Stuffing

*Use for poultry or
pork chops.*

Makes about 2½ cups

2 cups cooked brown rice, cooled
4 ounces Chinese sausage (lop
cheong), thinly sliced
4 or 5 water chestnuts, thinly sliced
3 dried shiitake mushrooms,
soaked, drained and diced

2 green onions, thinly sliced
1 tablespoon soy sauce
Freshly ground pepper

Combine rice, sausage, water chestnuts, mushrooms and onion in large bowl and mix well. Season with soy sauce and pepper. Chill until ready to use.

7 ❦ Meat

Meat has traditionally been more of a supporting player in oriental than in Western cooking. It is often not the centerpiece of the meal, and it seldom appears in the form of roasts or steaks. The fact is that Asian chefs have for centuries been serving meat just as modern dietary experts recommend: in moderate portions, typically accompanied by plentiful quantities of vegetables and rice. The result is a colorful, varied and eminently healthful repertoire of meat-based dishes.

Busy cooks will appreciate Flash-fried Lamb with Green Onions (page 94) and Thai Spicy Fried Ginger Beef (page 88); as with the other stir-fries in the chapter, the ingredients can be prepared ahead of time and cooked just moments before serving. But there's also a great selection of party recipes here. Thai Green Mango and Pork Platter (page 96), Korean Grilled Beef Slices (page 89), Peking Pork in Pancakes (page 99), and S.T. Ting Wong's Fried Fragrant Bells (page 97) are great selections for a pan-Asian buffet. Pork and Bitter Melon Stew (page 95), Sliced Pork in Flaky Sesame Pastries (page 96), Mu Shu Beef in Peking Pancakes (page 86), and Korean Grilled Short Ribs (page 87) will serve a sizable group, especially when accompanied by other dishes in typical Asian style.

From the Himalayas to the torrid Philippines, oriental cooking boasts a panoply of unique meat dishes—some festive and elaborate, others ideal for quick family suppers. The recipes provided here will give you a good idea of the pleasures that each of these distinctive cuisines has to offer.

Beef and Lamb

Mu Shu Beef in Peking Pancakes

A great main dish for an informal Chinese buffet. Allow guests to do their own final assembly.

Makes enough filling for 20 pancakes

2 teaspoons heavy soy sauce
2 teaspoons dry Sherry
1 teaspoon oriental sesame oil
½ teaspoon cornstarch
8 ounces flank steak or top sirloin (trimmed of all fat), cut into thin slivers (hold knife against grain)

14 golden needles (dried lily buds)
4 dried black mushrooms
¼ cup cloud ears
2 cups slivered green cabbage
4 green onions, coarsely chopped or slivered into 3-inch lengths

Sauce
3 tablespoons chicken stock
2 tablespoons dry Sherry

1 teaspoon heavy soy sauce
½ teaspoon oriental sesame oil
½ teaspoon sugar
¼ teaspoon salt
¼ teaspoon freshly ground pepper

4 eggs, beaten to blend
½ teaspoon oriental sesame oil
3 tablespoons peanut oil

2 garlic cloves, finely minced
⅓ to ½ teaspoon finely minced fresh ginger
1 tablespoon cornstarch mixed with 1½ teaspoons cold water

¾ to 1 cup hoisin sauce
20 Peking Pancakes*

Mix soy sauce, Sherry, oil and cornstarch in medium bowl. Add beef and mix well. Marinate at least 2 hours.

Soak golden needles, black mushrooms and cloud ears in separate bowls in enough hot water to cover. Let stand until softened, about 20 to 45 minutes. Drain well. Rinse under cold water and drain again, squeezing out excess moisture. Discard nobby ends of golden needles and cut remainder in half. Transfer to large bowl. Discard stems of mushrooms and cut caps into slivers. Add to golden needles. Blend in cloud ears, slivered green cabbage and onion and mix well. Set aside.

For sauce: Combine all ingredients for sauce in bowl and mix well. Set aside.

Combine eggs and sesame oil in medium bowl and mix well. Heat wok to very hot. Add 1 tablespoon peanut oil around sides. Add egg mixture and scramble just until set. Tip out onto plate and cover with wok top.

Return wok to high heat. Add another tablespoon peanut oil. Add undrained beef mixture and stir-fry until meat loses pink color. Tip out onto eggs and cover plate with wok top.

Return wok to high heat. Add remaining 1 tablespoon peanut oil with garlic and ginger. Immediately add cabbage mixture and stir-fry until cabbage turns bright green. Pour sauce around sides of wok. Return beef and eggs to wok (break eggs into smaller pieces if necessary). Add small amount of cornstarch mixture to thicken. Taste and adjust seasoning. Turn into dish.

Spread about 2 teaspoons hoisin sauce across center of each pancake. Add about ¼ cup mu shu filling. Roll into cylinders and serve immediately.

*Peking Pancakes

Makes about 20

2 cups unbleached all purpose flour
1 cup boiling water

½ cup oriental sesame oil

Measure flour into large bowl. Make well in center. Slowly pour boiling water into well and mix until flour forms loose mass (do not use processor). Turn out onto lightly floured surface. Knead until smooth, about 5 minutes. Cover dough with dry cloth and let rest for 30 minutes.

Roll dough out from center (do not roll over edges) on lightly floured surface to thickness of about 1/8 inch. Cut into circles using 2- or 3-inch round cutter. Press scraps together. Roll and cut again until all dough is shaped.

Rub smooth surface with some of sesame oil. Rub about 1 teaspoon oil over top of 1 round. Lay another round over top. With palm of hand, gently press together. Roll out from center until about 6 inches in diameter. Repeat with remaining rounds.

Heat heavy large ungreased skillet over medium-low heat. Place pancake in skillet and cook about 40 seconds on each side; if brown spots appear, reduce heat. Remove pancake from skillet. Carefully separate by pulling apart. Transfer to plate and cover with towel. Repeat process, stacking pancakes on plate as they are cooked. Wrap in foil or plastic and refrigerate or freeze until ready to use.

Fold each pancake in half, then in half again to form wedge shape. Overlap wedges on heat resistant plate or layer of aluminum foil. Bring water to vigorous boil in steamer (preferably Chinese). Transfer plate of pancakes to steamer rack. Cover and cook 8 minutes. Serve pancakes immediately.

Kahlbi Ribs

6 to 8 servings

5 to 6 pounds beef short ribs, cut into 3/4-inch strips
4 cups water
1 1/2 cups soy sauce
1 cup sugar
10 medium garlic cloves, chopped
4 green onions, trimmed and chopped

3 tablespoons sesame seeds
3 tablespoons oriental sesame oil
2 tablespoons chopped fresh ginger
1 tablespoon honey
2 teaspoons hot pepper sauce

Arrange ribs in deep roasting pan. Combine all remaining ingredients in large bowl and blend well. Pour over ribs. Cover and marinate in refrigerator 24 to 48 hours, turning ribs occasionally (longer time will result in spicier ribs).

Preheat broiler or prepare charcoal grill. Cook ribs to desired degree of doneness, turning once. Serve immediately.

Korean Grilled Short Ribs

6 main-course or 10 buffet servings

6 large meaty short ribs (trimmed of all fat), cut into 6-inch lengths for main-course servings or 3-inch lengths for buffet

Marinade
1/2 cup dark soy sauce
3 tablespoons vinegar

2 tablespoons vegetable oil
4 garlic cloves, crushed
2 green onions, finely chopped
1 tablespoon dry mustard
1 teaspoon grated fresh ginger
Pinch of freshly ground pepper

Score meat deeply crosswise at 1/4- to 1/2-inch intervals using sharp knife; score once lengthwise (this allows meat to absorb marinade better and cook more evenly). Arrange in shallow pan.

Combine marinade ingredients. Pour over ribs and let marinate at least 2 hours, turning frequently.

Prepare hibachi or barbecue, or preheat broiler. Cook ribs 3 to 4 inches from heat source, *without basting*, until crisp and browned, about 8 to 10 minutes on each side. Serve immediately.

Thai Spicy Fried Ginger Beef (Pad Neua Gaeng On)

Serve with steamed long-grain white rice.

4 servings

1 pound lean beef (top round or sirloin), thinly sliced and cut into 1/2 × 2-inch strips
3 tablespoons peanut oil
4 medium garlic cloves, thinly sliced
4 green serrano chilies, seeded and slivered
3 green onions, cut diagonally into 1/2-inch pieces

1 2-inch piece fresh ginger, cut julienne
1 tablespoon fresh lime juice
1 tablespoon fish sauce (nam pla)
1 teaspoon sugar
1 tablespoon cilantro leaves, minced

Pat meat dry. Heat oil in wok over medium-high heat. Add garlic and stir-fry until lightly golden. Add chilies, green onion and ginger and stir-fry until just browned, about 1 minute. Blend in lime juice, fish sauce and sugar. Arrange in heated dish. Sprinkle with cilantro. Serve immediately.

Dry Fried Beef

6 to 8 servings

2 cups corn or peanut oil (for frying)
2 pounds round steak or flank steak, trimmed, cut against grain into slices 1/8 inch thick
1 tablespoon sugar
1/2 teaspoon soy sauce
1/4 teaspoon salt

2 small hot red chilies, shredded
1 tablespoon shredded peeled ginger
1 green onion, chopped
1 garlic clove, minced
1 tablespoon oriental sesame oil
1 teaspoon rice vinegar
Freshly cooked rice

Heat 2 cups oil in wok or heavy large skillet to 350°F. Add beef in batches and fry 15 seconds. Transfer to bowl using slotted spoon. Stir sugar, soy sauce and salt into meat. Strain oil. Wipe wok clean. Return enough oil to wok to coat bottom. Place over medium heat. Add chilies, ginger, onion and garlic and stir 1 minute. Add meat and stir until mixture is dry, about 30 seconds. Stir in sesame oil and vinegar. Serve immediately with freshly steamed rice.

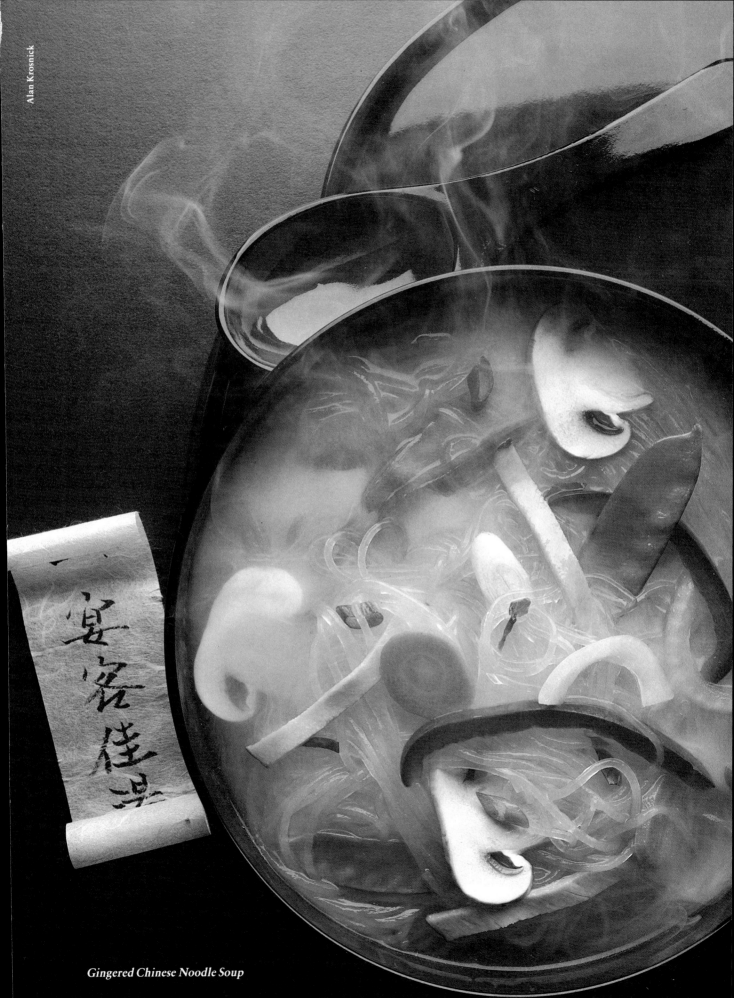

Gingered Chinese Noodle Soup

Left to right: Telor Bumbu Bali (Bali Egg); Pisang Goreng (Batter-fried Plantain); Kroket Ayam (Spicy Chicken Croquettes); Dadar Kepiting (Scrambled Eggs with Crabmeat)

Com Am Phu (Hué Rice)

Irwin Horowitz

Clockwise from top: Batayaki
(Beef in Sake and Soy Sauce);
Gohan (Japanese Steamed
Rice); Chawan Mushi
(Chicken and Shrimp Steamed
in Custard); Su No Mono
(Vinegared Broccoli Salad)

Mu Shu Beef in Peking Pancakes

Clockwise from top:
Cucumber Salad, Soy-smoked
Fish, Shanghai Radish Salad,
Cold Beef Shank with Five Spices
and (center) Tea Eggs

Top: *Macadamia Nut Torte*
Bottom: *Papaya Sorbet with Coconut Praline*

J. Barry O'Rourke

Peking Sesame Beef

4 to 6 servings

1 tablespoon soy sauce
1 tablespoon water
1½ teaspoons dry white wine
¼ teaspoon baking soda
1 1-pound flank steak or beef tenderloin (trimmed of fat), cut across grain into ½-inch slices

8 cups water
2 teaspoons salt
1 pound watercress

3 cups vegetable oil (for frying)
3 tablespoons cornstarch

1½ teaspoons chopped green onion
½ teaspoon chopped garlic
½ teaspoon chopped fresh ginger
3 tablespoons water
3 tablespoons soy sauce
1 tablespoon oriental sesame oil
1½ teaspoon sugar
¼ teaspoon freshly ground pepper
2 tablespoons sesame seeds
1½ teaspoons vegetable oil

Mix 1 tablespoon soy sauce, 1 tablespoon water, wine and baking soda in large bowl. Add beef and marinate for 1 hour.

Meanwhile, boil water with salt in medium saucepan. Add watercress and blanch 1 minute. Drain well. Let cool on paper towels. Transfer to serving platter.

Heat 3 cups oil in wok over medium-high heat. Add cornstarch to beef and blend well. Add beef to wok and fry 2 minutes. Remove with slotted spoon; drain on paper towels.

Discard all but 3 tablespoons oil from wok. Reheat oil over medium-high heat. Add green onion, garlic and ginger and stir-fry until fragrant. Add 3 tablespoons water, 3 tablespoons soy sauce, sesame oil, sugar and pepper and bring to boil. Stir in beef and sesame seeds and cook over high heat until sauce is almost evaporated. Add remaining 1½ teaspoons oil and toss lightly to mix. Spoon over watercress and serve.

Korean Grilled Beef Slices (Bulgogi)

4 main-course or 100 buffet servings

Marinade
6 green onions, finely chopped
5 large garlic cloves, crushed
½ cup dark soy sauce
2 tablespoons vegetable oil
2 tablespoons firmly packed brown sugar
2 tablespoons saké or dry Sherry

2 tablespoons toasted white sesame seeds
Freshly ground pepper

2 pounds boneless sirloin, chuck or flank steak (cut 1 to 2 inches thick), sliced ¼-inch thick across grain

Combine all marinade ingredients in shallow pan and mix well. Add meat, turning to coat completely. Let marinate at least 1 hour.

Prepare hibachi or barbecue. Grill meat on both sides to desired doneness. Serve immediately.

Zesty Hunan Beef

4 servings

1/4 cup soy sauce
2 tablespoons dry Sherry
2 garlic cloves, minced
1 pound lean beef round, sliced
  into 3 × 1/4-inch strips

1/4 cup vegetable oil
4 cups broccoli florets
3 1/2 cups sliced mushrooms
1 cup thinly sliced carrots

5 green onions, cut into
  1-inch pieces
1/4 cup toasted slivered almonds
2 tablespoons finely chopped
  fresh ginger
3/4 teaspoon dried red pepper flakes
2 tablespoons cornstarch dissolved
  in 1 tablespoon water
  Freshly cooked rice

Combine soy sauce, Sherry and garlic in large bowl. Add beef strips. Cover and marinate at room temperature 1 hour or in refrigerator overnight.

Drain beef, reserving marinade. Heat oil in large skillet or wok over high heat. Add beef and stir-fry 2 minutes. Remove from skillet; set aside. Add broccoli, mushrooms, carrots, green onions, almonds, ginger and pepper flakes to skillet and cook 2 minutes. Stir in reserved marinade and cornstarch. Cook until vegetables are crisp-tender and sauce thickens, 4 to 6 minutes. Return beef to skillet and heat through, 1 to 2 minutes. Serve immediately over rice.

Steamed Buns with Teriyaki Steak Filling

Makes 16

1/4 cup teriyaki sauce
1 tablespoon chopped onion
1 garlic clove, minced
1/2 teaspoon finely chopped
  fresh ginger
  Freshly ground pepper
1 pound sirloin tip, sliced into
  2 × 1/4-inch strips

2 tablespoons vegetable oil
2 cups chopped broccoli florets

3/4 cup shredded carrot
3/4 cup boiling water
4 teaspoons soy sauce
1 tablespoon dry vermouth
1 teaspoon crumbled beef
  bouillon cubes
2 tablespoons cornstarch

2 8-ounce packages refrigerator
  crescent dinner rolls

Combine first 5 ingredients in large bowl. Add meat to marinade and stir to coat well. Cover and refrigerate overnight.

Heat oil in wok or large skillet over medium-high heat. Add meat with marinade and stir until just browned, 1 to 2 minutes. Remove meat using slotted spoon; set aside. Add broccoli and carrot to wok and stir until broccoli is crisp-tender, about 2 minutes. Add boiling water, soy sauce, vermouth and bouillon. Return to boil. Add cornstarch and stir until sauce begins to thicken. Return meat to wok and cook until heated through. Remove from heat. (*Can be prepared 1 day ahead, covered and refrigerated. Bring to room temperature before using.*)

Open dough flat on lightly floured surface. Cut each rectangle in half crosswise, forming 8 squares. Roll squares out to thickness of 1/8 inch. Place about 3 tablespoons meat mixture in center of each. Fold points of square into center to enclose filling; pinch seams to seal. Place each bun on small piece of waxed paper, seam side down. In batches, arrange several buns about 1 inch apart in bamboo steamer set over boiling water. Cover and steam 10 minutes. Carefully remove from steamer. Peel off waxed paper. Serve immediately.

Sukiyaki

The ingredients for suki-yaki can be as exotic or as simple as you like. Arrange the platter of ingredients attractively, paying particular attention to the shape and color of the foods and how the flavors will complement each other. Prepare the sauce first and have it waiting in a small pitcher near the table. If possible, cook sukiyaki tableside in an electric skillet. You may also prepare it in the kitchen, although it won't be quite as impressive a presentation.

Serves 2

Cooking Sauce
- ¼ cup soy sauce
- ¼ cup beef stock
- 2 tablespoons water
- 2 tablespoons saké or dry Sherry
- 2 teaspoons sugar

- 1 small piece beef suet *or* 2 tablespoons oil

- 8 ounces beef filet or sirloin steak, cut into paper-thin slices
- 2 whole green onions, split lengthwise and cut into 1-inch pieces
- 1 small white onion, thinly sliced
- 2 celery stalks, sliced diagonally
- 2 ounces mushrooms, thinly sliced

- ¼ pound fresh spinach, stems removed, cut crosswise into 1-inch strips
- 2 ounces shirataki (noodlelike threads, available canned), cooked and drained, *or* 2 ounces thin spaghetti, cooked and drained
- 2 ounces tofu, cut into ½-inch cubes *or* one 1-egg omelet, cooled and cut into ½-inch strips
- 2 eggs, lightly beaten (optional)

Combine all ingredients for cooking sauce in small bowl and blend well. (If cooking at table, transfer to small pitcher for easier handling.)

Heat electric skillet to 375°F, or place large skillet on burner over medium-high heat. Using chopsticks or a long fork, rub suet around skillet until it melts, or film the pan with oil. When skillet is very hot, add beef and stir-fry until it loses pink color; *do not brown.* Push beef to one side and begin adding all vegetables except spinach in order given, stir-frying each briefly and keeping in separate piles. Add cooking sauce and allow to simmer uncovered for approximately 4 minutes.

Push each pile of vegetables to edges of pan and add spinach, pressing it down into liquid and turning frequently. When wilted, form into a mound. Add shirataki or spaghetti and tofu, turning gently to allow them to absorb flavors of broth. If using omelet strips, add them just before serving. Transfer to heated plates, dividing evenly. Drain off remaining cooking sauce and serve separately, or dip each bite into raw egg before eating, as is traditional.

Oriental-style Beef and Noodles

Flash freezing meat for 45 minutes will make slicing easy. Use the microwave to make preparing this dish even easier.

2 to 3 servings

- ½ pound flank steak
- 2 tablespoons soy sauce
- 1½ teaspoons cornstarch
- 2 tablespoons oil
- 2 teaspoons freshly grated ginger
- ½ teaspoon sugar

- 2 cups hot water
- 6 ounces fresh or frozen snow peas (thawed)

- 1 cup shredded Chinese cabbage (bok choy)
- 1 cup fresh bean sprouts
- 1 3-ounce package instant oriental style noodles (with seasoning packet)

Slice steak in half lengthwise; cut crosswise into slices ¼ inch thick. Combine soy sauce and cornstarch in 11-inch oval baking or gratin dish and stir until cornstarch dissolves. Add oil, ginger and sugar and mix well. Stir in beef. Marinate 30 to 45 minutes.

Bring water just to boil in 8-cup measure on High, about 5 to 6 minutes. Add snow peas, cabbage, bean sprouts and noodles (with seasoning packet) and mix well. Cook on High 3 minutes. Turn into serving dish and set aside. Cook beef on High, stirring once, just until meat loses its pink color, about 2 to 3 minutes; do not overcook. Spoon over noodles and vegetables.

Beef in Saké and Soy Sauce (Batayaki)

4 servings

Sauce
1 cup saké or dry Sherry
½ cup Japanese soy sauce
1 tablespoon rice vinegar
¼ teaspoon tōgarashi (dried hot red peppers) or cayenne pepper
Sugar to taste (optional)

Batayaki
1 pound top sirloin, thinly siced
2 onions, cut into ¼-inch slices
1 medium daikon (Japanese white radish), cut into ¼-inch-thick slices
1 medium cucumber, thinly sliced

1 whole bamboo shoot, thinly sliced
8 green onions, cut into 1-inch lengths
Optional ingredients:
  Sliced tofu
  Sliced mushrooms
  Fresh spinach, coarsely torn
  Cooked shirataki (Japanese cellophane noodles or yam noodles)

¼ cup (½ stick) butter

For sauce: Combine all ingredients and blend well. Divide evenly among small individual serving dishes.

For batayaki: Arrange beef, onion, daikon, cucumber, bamboo shoot, green onion and any desired optional ingredients on large platter.

Melt butter in sukiyaki pan or electric skillet over high heat. Add vegetables, in batches if necessary, and stir-fry until partially cooked, about 5 minutes. Move vegetables to side of pan. Add beef and sauté to desired doneness. Mix vegetables with meat. Turn into dish and serve immediately with sauce.

Tibetan Stir-fry of Tongue, Ginger and Chilies (Chelay)

Serve this very spicy dish over freshly steamed rice.

6 servings

1 2- to 2½-pound beef or veal tongue
6 cups water
½ teaspoon salt

1 tablespoon corn oil or peanut oil
¼ cup thinly sliced onion

1 teaspoon minced garlic
1 teaspoon minced fresh ginger
½ teaspoon dried red pepper flakes
2 tablespoons light soy sauce

Simmer tongue in water and salt over medium heat until tender, 2 to 2½ hours. Peel off skin and discard. Cut into ¼-inch-thick slices. Reserve 2 tablespoons cooking liquid.

Heat oil in heavy medium skillet over medium heat. Add onion, garlic, ginger and pepper flakes and stir 2 minutes. Add tongue, soy sauce and reserved cooking liquid and stir for 3 minutes. Serve immediately.

🍏 Japan at Your Table

Japanese cuisine has attracted a multitude of fans, both for its nutritional value and for its remarkable artistry. In Japan, more than in almost any other country in the world, the presentation of food is an art form. If you're uncertain about your flair for artistic table arrangement, make construction paper cutouts to represent each dish in the menu. Place the different "dishes" where you think they look most attractive, and use them as a guide for the final presentation. A few more tips when preparing Japanese foods:

- Use corn oil, peanut oil, or a combination of vegetable oils when frying. The Japanese use vegetable oils almost exclusively. Oriental sesame oil is sometimes used sparingly as a flavoring in the vegetable oil.

- Oil temperature is very important. The oil is ready when it bubbles around a dry wooden chopstick.

- Used oil may be cooled, strained and refrigerated for further use.

- Although a wok is not traditional, using it conserves oil, since you can use much less oil than in a flat pan.

- Drain fried foods on a rack covered with paper towels.

- When beating eggs with chopsticks, use four chopsticks to speed the work. And use long chopsticks when cooking in deep oil; they help keep you from being spattered.

- In order to make decorative vegetable flowers and leaves easily, always use a razor-sharp knife.

- When cutting dried noodles, put noodles in a paper bag and cut with scissors to avoid scattering pieces; or chop in processor fitted with steel knife.

- In Japan there is a right and wrong side to food. For instance, when a whole fish is presented on a platter, the "right" side is with the head to the left and the belly toward you, the tail to the right. With fish steaks and chicken breasts, skin side up is the "right" side. When broiling, broil the "wrong" side first, then turn and finish on the right side.

- In setting forth a Japanese meal, the following order is prescribed: rice bowl to the left, soup to the right, featured dish in the center just behind these, and side dishes and pickles to right and left behind main dish. Sauces and condiments are placed close to the dishes with which they belong, and the chopsticks are directly in front of the diner, always pointing to the left and frequently resting on a small "pillow" of porcelain to keep tips off the table.

- As in most present-day nouvelle cuisine, most Japanese dishes are served at room temperature or lukewarm for the best flavor emphasis.

- Courtesy and consideration for others prevails in Japanese culture, and this extends to meals as well. Begin the meal by saying "Itadakimasu" which, said before eating, means "I receive." When you have finished, politely say, "Gochisō sama deshita," which means, "I have been royally feasted." And so you will be.

Flash-fried Lamb with Green Onions

2 servings

2 tablespoons peanut oil
2 tablespoons rice wine or
  dry Sherry
3 tablespoons light soy sauce
½ teaspoon salt
½ teaspoon ground Szechwan
  peppercorns
12 ounces lamb (from shoulder or
  leg), sliced ⅛ inch thick

1 tablespoon rice vinegar
1 tablespoon oriental sesame oil
½ cup peanut oil
3 garlic cloves, minced
4 green onions, cut crosswise
  into 3 pieces and lengthwise
  into shreds
  Freshly cooked rice

Blend 2 tablespoons peanut oil, rice wine, 2 tablespoons soy sauce, salt and peppercorns in medium bowl. Add lamb and marinate at room temperature for 15 to 20 minutes.

Combine remaining 1 tablespoon soy sauce, vinegar and sesame oil in small bowl. Drain lamb; pat dry. Heat remaining ½ cup peanut oil in wok or heavy large skillet over high heat until hot but not smoking. Stir in garlic. Add lamb and sear on both sides. Add vinegar mixture and green onions and stir to heat through. Serve immediately with freshly steamed rice.

Indonesian Lamb with Cold Peanut Sauce

4 servings

¾ cup oil
⅓ cup diced celery
⅓ cup diced onion
1 garlic clove, minced
½ cup prepared mustard
¼ cup cider vinegar
3 tablespoons curry powder
3 tablespoons honey

2 bay leaves
2 teaspoons A-1 sauce
1 teaspoon oregano
2 dashes hot pepper sauce
  Juice and peel of 1 large lemon

2 racks of lamb, fat trimmed

  Cold Peanut Sauce*

Heat oil in medium skillet over medium heat. Add celery, onion and garlic and sauté until onion is transparent. Reduce heat, stir in all remaining ingredients except lamb and peanut sauce and simmer briefly until heated through. Pour into bowl and cool slightly. Cover and refrigerate 2 hours to allow flavors to blend.

Transfer marinade to large shallow baking dish or pan. Add lamb, turning several times to coat. Cover and marinate in refrigerator 3 to 4 hours.

Place rack in center of oven and preheat to 550°F. Grease shallow baking pan. Drain marinade from meat and set aside. Wrap lamb in foil, leaving meaty portions exposed. Place in pan and brush with some of reserved marinade. For medium rare, bake 15 minutes total, turning once and basting frequently with remaining marinade. (Exact cooking time will depend on thickness of meat and desired doneness.) Serve immediately with Cold Peanut Sauce.

*Cold Peanut Sauce

Makes about 1 cup

½ cup creamy style peanut butter,
  room temperature
½ cup coconut cream
2 tablespoons soy sauce

1½ teaspoons Worcestershire sauce
¼ teaspoon salt
  Dash of hot pepper sauce
  Juice of ¼ large lemon

Combine all ingredients in small mixing bowl and blend thoroughly. Cover and chill. Serve cold.

 *Pork*

Cashew Papaya Pork

Serve with fried rice, steamed broccoli and a crisp, dry Sauvignon Blanc, Fumé Blanc or a fruity Zinfandel.

6 servings

1 cup all purpose flour
¾ cup water
2 eggs, beaten to blend
1 teaspoon salt
1½ pounds lean boneless pork, well dried and cubed
Peanut or safflower oil for frying

½ cup red wine vinegar
¼ cup firmly packed brown sugar
½ cup pineapple juice
¼ cup cornstarch
1 papaya, peeled, seeded and diced
½ cup toasted cashews

Mix flour, ¼ cup water, eggs and salt in large bowl; batter will be thick. Add pork and toss until well coated. Heat oil in large skillet over medium-high heat. Add pork in batches and fry until brown and crisp on all sides. Remove pork from skillet using slotted spoon. Drain on paper towels.

Combine remaining ½ cup water with vinegar and brown sugar in medium saucepan and bring to boil over medium-high heat, stirring occasionally. Meanwhile, blend pineapple juice and cornstarch. Stir into vinegar mixture and continue cooking until thickened. Gently stir in pork, papaya and cashews, being careful not to mash papaya. Serve immediately.

Pork and Bitter Melon Stew (Pakbet)

The melon lends distinctive flavor to this Filipino specialty.

12 servings

2 tablespoons vegetable oil
3 tablespoons shrimp paste (bagoong) or one 2-ounce can anchovies, drained and minced
4 medium garlic cloves, pounded to paste in mortar with pestle
2 medium tomatoes, chopped
1 medium onion, chopped
1½ pounds ½-inch-thick pork loin chops, boned and cut into 2 × 2-inch pieces

1 small eggplant, halved lengthwise and cut crosswise into ½-inch slices
1 8-inch-long bitter melon, halved lengthwise, seeded and cut crosswise into ¼-inch slices
1 cup small okra pods, trimmed

12 ounces spinach, stemmed

Heat oil in wok or heavy large skillet over medium heat. Add shrimp paste and garlic and stir 5 minutes. Mix in tomatoes and onion and stir-fry until tender, about 8 minutes. Add pork and cook until no longer pink, about 15 minutes, stirring frequently. Mix in eggplant and bitter melon. Cover and simmer until melon turns bright green, about 5 minutes. Add okra. Cover and simmer until vegetables are crisp-tender, about 5 minutes.

Arrange spinach atop mixture. Cover and cook until spinach wilts, about 2 minutes. Transfer pork to center of heated platter. Surround with cooked melon and vegetables and serve.

Thai Green Mango and Pork Platter

For a special presentation, garnish this with slices of yellow and green mango.

10 buffet servings

2 tablespoons vegetable oil
½ cup thinly sliced shallots
4 medium garlic cloves, thinly sliced
18 ounces ground pork
2 tablespoons fish sauce (nam pla)
1 tablespoon dried shrimp, coarsely ground in blender
1 teaspoon salt

¼ teaspoon freshly ground pepper
Pinch of sugar
3 tablespoons roasted unsalted peanuts, crushed
1½ pounds green mango, thinly sliced
¼ cup cilantro leaves, chopped
Fresh red chilies, seeded and slivered (optional)

Heat oil in heavy large skillet over medium heat. Add shallots and garlic and cook until golden brown, stirring frequently. Remove mixture using slotted spoon and drain on paper towels. Add pork to skillet, crumble with fork and cook until just brown. Blend in fish sauce, shrimp, salt, pepper and sugar. Remove from heat and stir in peanuts. Mix in mango. Turn out onto platter. Toss with shallot mixture. Garnish with cilantro and fresh red chilies. Serve immediately.

Cantonese Roast Pork Tenderloin

6 main-course or 10 buffet servings

Marinade
¼ cup dark soy sauce
3 tablespoons hoisin sauce
1 tablespoon dry Sherry
2 garlic cloves, minced
1 teaspoon grated fresh ginger

1 teaspoon firmly packed brown sugar
Salt

1 3-pound boneless whole pork tenderloin

Combine all ingredients for marinade in small bowl. Arrange pork in shallow pan and pour marinade over. Let stand at room temperature about 4 hours, turning occasionally; refrigerate in pan if marinating longer.

Prepare hibachi or barbecue, or preheat broiler. Cook meat 4 inches from heat source, turning and basting several times, until crisp, browned and cooked through, about 40 minutes. Slice pork thinly and serve immediately.

Sliced Pork in Flaky Sesame Pastries

Serve Chinese mustard with these tasty oriental "hamburgers."

Makes 12

2 12-ounce pork tenderloins
2 tablespoons dark soy sauce

⅓ cup vegetable oil

4½ teaspoons sugar
3 cups chicken stock

Flaky Sesame Pastries*

Coat pork with soy sauce. Wrap tightly and refrigerate at least 2 hours. (*Can be prepared 1 day ahead.*)

Pat pork dry. Heat vegetable oil in wok over medium heat. Add sugar and stir until caramelized and bubbling, about 1½ minutes. Carefully add pork (mixture will spatter). Cover and cook until pork is rich mahogany brown, turning occasionally, 10 to 15 minutes. Remove pork from wok. Pour out oil then return pork to wok. Add stock, cover and simmer until pork is cooked through, turning occasionally, about 12 minutes. Transfer pork to platter. Simmer liquid until reduced to ⅓ cup. Cut pork across grain into thin slices. Top with cooking liquid. (*Can be prepared 1 day ahead. Cover with foil and refrigerate. Bring to room temperature, then reheat in 300°F oven until heated through, about 15 minutes.*)

Split pastries in half horizontally. Fill each with pork and some cooking liquid. Serve immediately.

*Flaky Sesame Pastries

Makes 12

3½ cups unbleached all purpose flour
3 tablespoons solid
  vegetable shortening
6 tablespoons clarified butter
¾ cup ice water

1 egg, beaten to blend
½ cup sesame seeds, toasted to
  light golden brown

⅔ to 1 cup vegetable oil

Combine 1¼ cups flour, vegetable shortening and 4 tablespoons clarified butter in processor. Blend until mixture forms ball. (Can also be mixed by hand.) Set aside. Combine remaining 2¼ cups flour, 2 tablespoons clarified butter and cold water in processor. Process until smooth, silky ball forms, about 30 seconds. (Can also be mixed by hand. Knead about 6 minutes.)

Flatten large dough ball into disc on lightly floured surface. Roll out to 8-inch-diameter round. Place smaller dough ball in center of round. Pull edges of round up to enclose dough ball completely. Pinch tightly to seal. Cover and let rest 10 minutes.

Turn dough seam side down on lightly floured surface. Roll out to 12 × 18-inch rectangle. Trim both 18-inch edges. Roll dough up tightly jelly roll fashion, starting at one long side. Roll between hands and surface to form 20-inch-long cylinder. Cut into 12 even pieces. Press center of 1 piece crosswise, tilting ends upward. Press ends together tightly, forming ball. Pinch to seal. Repeat with remaining dough.

Place 1 dough ball pinched side down on lightly floured surface. Roll out to 4-inch-diameter circle. Repeat with remaining dough. Brush top of each with egg and dip in sesame seeds.

Heat 2 tablespoons oil in heavy 12-inch skillet over medium-high heat. Add 4 dough circles sesame sides up. Cover and cook until bottoms brown and pastries puff, 3 to 4 minutes, reducing heat if browning too quickly. Turn pastries over and add more oil if necessary. Reduce heat to low, cover and cook until second side is golden brown, about 8 minutes. Drain on paper towels. Wipe out pan and add more oil. Repeat with remaining pastries and vegetable oil. (*Can be prepared 4 hours ahead. Wrap tightly.*)

Preheat oven to 300°F. Arrange pastries on baking sheet. Heat in oven for about 10 minutes. Serve warm.

S. T. Ting Wong's Fried Fragrant Bells (Chinese Crisp-fried Bean Curd)

Makes about 40 to 45

1 pound ground pork,
  veal or chicken
2 green onions, finely chopped
1 slice fresh ginger, minced
3 tablespoons chicken stock
1 tablespoon dark soy sauce
1 tablespoon dry Sherry or Chinese
  rice wine
1 egg
2 tablespoons cornstarch
3 tablespoons water

4 dried bean curd sheets
  Additional cornstarch

Peppercorn Salt (optional)
¼ cup salt
2 tablespoons Szechwan
  peppercorns

2 to 4 cups vegetable oil

Combine pork, onion, ginger, stock, soy sauce, Sherry, egg and 1 tablespoon cornstarch in bowl and mix well. Combine remaining 1 tablespoon cornstarch with water in small bowl.

Moisten 1 bean curd sheet under running water. Place on work surface and spread with ¼ of meat mixture. Roll as for jelly roll; brush long edge with dissolved cornstarch to seal. Repeat to make three more rolls. Cut each into slices 1½ inches thick; dip each end in additional cornstarch to seal filling. (*Can be done 3 to 4 hours ahead to this point and refrigerated.*)

For salt: Combine salt and peppercorns in small skillet and cook until browned. Crush in mortar with pestle.

Heat oil in wok or deep fryer to 375°F. Add slices a few at a time and fry until crisp. Drain on paper towels. Serve hot with peppercorn salt, if desired.

Chinese-style Ribs

2 servings

2 pounds spareribs, cut into individual ribs
¼ cup soy sauce
2 slices fresh ginger
2 green onions, cut into ½-inch pieces
2 whole star anise

2 tablespoons honey
2 tablespoons dry Sherry
2 garlic cloves, finely minced
2 teaspoons sugar
1 teaspoon salt
½ teaspoon five-spice powder or ground allspice

Basting Sauce:
¼ cup soy sauce

Combine ribs in large saucepan with enough water to cover. Add soy sauce, ginger, onion and star anise. Bring to boil over medium-high heat, then reduce heat and simmer 20 minutes. Drain well. *Ribs can be made ahead to this point and refrigerated. Bring to room temperature before broiling or barbecuing.*

For basting sauce: Combine all ingredients in small bowl and blend until sugar is thoroughly dissolved.

Preheat broiler or prepare barbecue grill. Broil ribs 5 to 6 inches from heat source until ribs are well browned and nicely glazed, turning and basting frequently. Serve immediately.

Orange Barbecued Spareribs

2 servings

2 pounds spareribs, cut into individual ribs
¼ cup soy sauce
2 slices fresh ginger
2 green onions, cut into ½-inch pieces
2 whole star anise

Basting Sauce:
½ cup chicken stock
½ cup sugar
2 tablespoons soy sauce
1 teaspoon finely chopped orange peel

Combine ribs in large saucepan with enough water to cover. Add soy sauce, ginger, onion and star anise. Bring to boil over medium-high heat, then reduce heat and simmer 20 minutes. Drain well. *Ribs can be made ahead to this point and refrigerated. Bring to room temperature before broiling or barbecuing.*

For basting sauce: Combine ingredients for sauce in small saucepan and bring to boil. Reduce heat and simmer 15 minutes, stirring occasionally.

Preheat broiler or prepare barbecue grill. Broil ribs 5 to 6 inches from heat source until ribs are well browned and nicely glazed, turning and basting frequently. Serve immediately.

Peking Pork in Pancakes

Succulent pork strips are enclosed in Chinese pancakes for this festive dish.

8 servings

Marinade
- ½ teaspoon cornstarch
- 1 teaspoon Chinese rice wine or dry Sherry
- 1 tablespoon beaten egg
  Pinch of salt
  Pinch of freshly ground white pepper

- 1 pound center-cut pork loin, partially frozen

- 2 cups vegetable oil (for frying)

- 4 tablespoons Hoisin Sauce Mixture*

- ¼ teaspoon (heaping) minced garlic
- 3 tablespoons plus 1½ teaspoons Kung Bao Sauce (see page 66)
- 1 tablespoon Cornstarch Mixture (see page 66)
- 1 tablespoon Chinese rice wine or dry Sherry
- 1 tablespoon oriental sesame oil
- ½ cup shredded green onions
  Chinese Pancakes
  Additional Hoisin Sauce Mixture

For marinade: Combine first 5 ingredients in medium bowl.

Slice pork across grain into ⅛-inch-thick slices using sharp knife. Stack slices and cut into ⅛-inch-thick matchsticks. Mix with marinade. Cover mixture and refrigerate at least 30 minutes or overnight.

Heat vegetable oil in wok or deep saucepan until bubbles form around dry wooden chopstick inserted in oil (about 350°F). Add pork and stir until no longer pink, about 20 seconds. Carefully pour pork mixture into colander set over large metal bowl.

Return 1 teaspoon oil to wok and heat. Add hoisin sauce mixture and garlic. Stir-fry until aromatic, 15 to 20 seconds. Mix in kung bao sauce, cornstarch mixture and pork. Stir-fry until sauce coats pork, about 30 seconds. Add wine and sesame oil and toss. Top with green onions. Spoon pork mixture into pancakes; roll pancakes to enclose filling. Serve immediately, passing additional sauce mixture separately.

*Hoisin Sauce Mixture

Makes about 1¼ cups

- 1 cup hoisin sauce
- 2 tablespoons Chinese rice wine or dry Sherry

- 2 tablespoons oriental sesame oil
- 4½ teaspoons sugar
- 1½ teaspoons rice vinegar

Combine all ingredients in bowl. (*Can be stored indefinitely in refrigerator.*)

*Chinese Pancakes

Makes 18

- 2¼ cups unbleached all purpose flour
- 2 tablespoons vegetable oil
- ⅛ teaspoon salt

- ⅔ cup boiling water

- 2 tablespoons oriental sesame oil

Combine 2¼ cups flour, vegetable oil and salt in processor. Add boiling water. Blend until mixture forms ball, then process until smooth and silky but not sticky, about 30 seconds. (Can also be made by hand. Knead dough 6 to 8 minutes.) Wrap in plastic and let stand 15 to 30 minutes.

Cut dough in half. Roll each half into 9-inch-long rope. Cut each into nine 1-inch pieces. Roll each piece of dough out on generously floured surface to 3-inch round. Generously brush tops of 2 rounds with sesame oil. Stack, placing oiled sides together. Repeat with remaining dough rounds, forming 9 double pancakes. Roll each double pancake out on floured surface to 8- to 9-inch-diameter $1/16$-inch thick round, turning over frequently.

Place baking sheet upside down over 2 burners set on medium-low heat. Cook 2 double pancakes until somewhat dry but still supple, reducing heat if necessary, about 30 seconds on each side; do not brown. Transfer to dry towel. Pull each double pancake apart into 2 thin pancakes. Arrange oiled side up on kitchen towel and cover with another towel. Repeat with remaining double pancakes. (*Can be prepared 3 days ahead. Cool completely. Wrap in plastic bag and refrigerate.*)

Bring water to boil in steamer. Reduce heat to medium. Stack pancakes on plate. Set on steamer rack. Cover and steam until hot, about 10 minutes.

Siamese Roast Pork with Thai Curry Paste

Thai curries differ sharply from others in their magical blending of pungent spices and fragrant herbs. These kaeng *curries are "color coded"—bright red, jungle green, turmeric yellow—according to their flavorings.*

6 servings

1 5-pound pork loin roast
Thai Curry Paste*
1 large pineapple

Basting Sauce
$1/3$ cup firmly packed brown sugar

$1/4$ cup soy sauce
$1/4$ cup white vinegar

Chopped fresh coriander

Prepare barbecue spit or smoke oven. Using skewer, poke several holes in meat. Rub curry paste over entire surface and into holes. Leaving pineapple whole, remove shell in one large piece and tie around top part of roast with heavy twine. Balance meat on spit or set in smoke oven and cook for 1 hour.

While roast is cooking, combine brown sugar, soy and vinegar and blend well. Cut whole pineapple into chunks.

After 1 hour, remove pineapple rind from roast and discard. Continue cooking meat, basting frequently, until thermometer inserted in thickest part registers 170°F, about 20 minutes. Transfer roast to platter. Toss pineapple with some of basting sauce, sprinkle with coriander and serve with meat.

*Thai Curry Paste

7 dried hot red chili
 peppers, seeded
2 green onions
2 garlic cloves
1 tablespoon dried shrimp
 (optional), soaked

1 tablespoon turmeric
1 teaspoon salt
1 teaspoon grated fresh ginger
 Juice of 1 lemon
 Zest of 1 lemon, grated

Mix all ingredients in food processor or blender until fairly smooth. (*For a green paste, substitute green chilies for red and add fresh coriander and parsley leaves to taste. For a red paste, substitute 1 tablespoon paprika for turmeric.*)

8 ❦ Desserts

Traditional Asian menus do not include dessert, at least not in the occidental sense of the word; a simple offering of fresh fruit is considered the best conclusion to a multicourse meal. Sweets are usually eaten as a snack, or perhaps served during a pause in a formal banquet. Most Westerners, however, prefer a separate dessert course, and the sampling of oriental-style sweets in this chapter effects a happy compromise between Eastern and Western tastes.

Ideas for fruit desserts are found throughout the Orient. Vietnamese Fruit Fantasy (page 102), a spectacular presentation, features fresh tropical fruits "sculpted" to resemble a whimsical flying fish. Of Japanese inspiration, Kumquat Jubilee (page 105) is an imaginative brew of liqueur-glazed fruit that is flambéed and spooned over ice cream.

Since many oriental entrées require last-minute preparation, a do-ahead dessert has special appeal—but there is no need to sacrifice elegance for convenience. Macadamia Nut Torte (page 110) and Papaya Sorbet with Coconut Praline (page 103) are a perfect pair on the buffet table. The sinfully rich torte, filled with pineapple, lime and rum, is well matched with the refreshing sorbet and its unique crunchy topping. For a smaller gathering, try the Tangerine Mousse on page 106—not classically oriental, perhaps, but a perfect grace note to any Asian menu. And what Chinese meal would be complete without almond cookies? Team the recipe on page 109 with Lemon Ginger Ice Cream (page 106) for the ideal finale to an oriental feast.

Vietnamese Fruit Fantasy

Use any combination of tropical fruits to create this delightful dessert. Flower, star, moon or other interesting shapes can be easily designed.

6 to 10 servings

1 fresh pineapple
1 8-ounce can lichees, drained and halved (about 7 to 8)
½ papaya, peeled, seeded and thinly sliced (reserve some seeds)
2 slivers tomato peel or red bell pepper

3 kiwis, peeled and sliced
1 8-ounce can mandarin oranges, drained (about 15 pieces)
Pineapple leaves (optional)

Remove crown from pineapple and set aside for decoration. Trim off ends and discard. Slice off brown outer layer using large sharp knife. Hold blade of knife directly against 1 row of "eyes" on 1 side of pineapple. Make a diagonal cut ½ inch deep into fruit; then make another diagonal cut against other side of "eyes." Remove wedge-shaped piece with eyes and discard. Repeat until all eyes have been removed and cuts in fruit give it spiral shape. Cut pineapple in half from crown to stem and remove core. Cut fruit into slices ½ inch thick; cut each slice in half.

Layer several pineapple slices at one end of large serving platter to form head of fish. Use 1 lichee half for eye and papaya seeds for pupil. Shape mouth with slivers of tomato or red pepper. Make scales and top half of fish by overlapping kiwi slices. Use halved lichee and mandarin oranges for belly. Arrange thin slices of papaya in fan shape for tail. If desired, snip pieces of pineapple leaves to make fins at top and bottom of fish. Cover loosely with plastic and refrigerate until serving time.

Japanese Kumquat Sauce

A delightful topping for ice cream, waffles or crepes. Adding 1½ ounces more pectin will make the sauce firm to a marmalade-like consistency.

Makes about 5 cups

1 pound kumquats, halved and seeded
2½ cups cold water
2 tablespoons saké

¼ cup fresh lemon juice
3 cups sugar
2 3-ounce pouches liquid pectin

Coarsely chop kumquats in processor using 1 or 2 on/off turns. Bring to boil with water and saké in heavy large saucepan. Reduce heat and simmer 2 minutes. Add lemon juice. Stir in sugar in 2 additions. Simmer 2 minutes. Increase heat and bring to rolling boil. Mix in pectin. Boil exactly 3 minutes, stirring occasionally. Immediately ladle sauce into sterilized jars and seal according to manufacturer's instructions. Refrigerate up to 6 months.

Gingered Pineapple

An easy do-ahead dessert.

6 servings

1 cup sour cream
¼ cup honey
3 tablespoons finely minced candied ginger

1 20-ounce can pineapple chunks, chilled and drained

Combine sour cream, honey and ginger in small bowl and refrigerate at least 30 minutes. When ready to serve, spoon pineapple chunks into bowls and top with sour cream mixture.

Peaches with Pistachio Cream

8 servings

Pistachio Cream
1⅓ cups shelled roasted unsalted pistachio nuts (about 12 ounces in shell)
6 to 7 tablespoons sugar
12 ounces Petit-Suisse triple crème cheese,* drained
½ teaspoon vanilla
¼ teaspoon almond extract
½ cup sour cream

Poached Peaches
4 large peaches, peeled and halved
1 750-ml bottle dry rosé

3 cups water
½ cup sugar
1 vanilla bean, split, or 2 teaspoons vanilla extract

Apricot Puree
7 ounces dried apricots
1½ cups dry rosé
Water
¼ cup sugar

2 kiwis, peeled and sliced

For pistachio cream: Blanch nuts in large pot of boiling water 2 minutes. Drain and rinse under cold water. Rub with coarse towel to remove skins. Reserve 3 tablespoons nuts for garnish. Combine remainder with 6 tablespoons sugar in processor and blend to paste. Transfer to bowl. Using electric mixer, blend in cheese, vanilla and almond extract. Fold in sour cream. Add remaining 1 tablespoon sugar if desired. Refrigerate at least 1 hour. (*Can be prepared up to 3 days ahead.*)

For peaches: Enlarge cavities in peaches slightly, using spoon. Cut flat on rounded sides to prevent tipping. Combine wine, water, sugar and vanilla in heavy large nonaluminum saucepan. Cook over low heat, swirling pan occasionally, until sugar dissolves. Increase heat and bring to boil. Reduce heat and simmer 5 minutes, stirring occasionally. Add peaches. Adjust heat so liquid barely shimmers and poach peaches until slightly tender, 3 to 5 minutes. Cool in syrup. Refrigerate 1 hour. (*Can be prepared up to 2 days ahead.*)

For apricot puree: Combine apricots, wine and enough water to cover fruit by 1 inch in heavy nonaluminum saucepan. Let stand until apricots soften, about 1 hour. Simmer until apricots break up, about 20 minutes, stirring frequently and adding water to cover if necessary. Add sugar and stir until dissolved. Cool slightly. Puree in processor, adding enough water to thin to consistency of whipping cream. Refrigerate 1 hour. (*Can be prepared up to 2 days ahead.*)

To assemble: Drain peaches on rack. Spread thin layer of apricot puree on each plate. Fill each peach half generously with pistachio cream. Arrange in center of plates. Garnish with kiwi. Coarsely chop reserved nuts. Sprinkle over top. Let stand at room temperature 20 minutes before serving.

*If unavailable, substitute 10 ounces fresh cream cheese thinned to smooth consistency with about ½ cup whipping cream.

Papaya Sorbet with Coconut Praline

12 servings

Coconut Praline
1 cup shredded unsweetened coconut
2 cups powdered sugar

Sorbet
3⅓ cups water
2⅓ cups sugar

10 large papayas (about 1 pound each), peeled and seeded
1⅓ cups fresh lime juice

For praline: Oil jelly roll pan. Stir coconut into wok or heavy large skillet over low heat until light brown and dry. Add sugar and stir until caramelized. Pour into pan. Cool until hard.

Break praline into 1-inch pieces. Chop coarsely in processor. (*Can be prepared 1 month ahead and frozen.*)

For sorbet: Heat 3 cups water and 2 cups sugar in heavy medium saucepan over low heat until sugar dissolves, swirling pan occasionally. Increase heat and boil until reduced to 4 cups. Cool.

Cut 8 papayas into 1-inch chunks. Puree in processor. Transfer to large bowl. Stir in syrup and 1 cup lime juice. Refrigerate until well chilled.

Transfer papaya mixture to ice cream maker and process according to manufacturer's instructions. (Sorbet can also be frozen in ice cube trays with dividers in place. When frozen, puree mixture in processor until smooth.)

Meanwhile, mix remaining ⅓ cup water, ⅓ cup sugar and ⅓ cup lime juice in medium bowl until sugar dissolves. Cut remaining 2 papayas lengthwise into ¾-inch-thick slices. Stir into lime juice mixture. Cover and refrigerate.

Scoop sorbet into large glass bowl. Cover tightly and freeze.

Just before serving, drain papaya, sprinkle with praline and place atop sorbet. Pass remaining praline.

Broiled Pears with Caramel Sauce

Serve any remaining caramel sauce over vanilla ice cream or pound cake for a quick and easy dessert.

4 servings

Sauce
⅔ cup sugar
3 tablespoons cold water
3 tablespoons hot water
1½ cups whipping cream
1 teaspoon vanilla
1 teaspoon chilled unsalted butter

Pears
2 large ripe pears
1 lemon, halved
2 tablespoons (¼ stick) butter, melted
Sugar

For sauce: Cook sugar and cold water in heavy small saucepan over low heat until sugar dissolves, swirling pan occasionally. Increase heat and bring to boil, washing down sides of pan with wet pastry brush. Boil until syrup becomes brown, watching carefully to prevent burning. Remove from heat. Add hot water (be careful; mixture may spatter). Add cream. Return pan to medium heat and boil until thickened, swirling pan occasionally, 6 to 8 minutes. Remove from heat. Stir in vanilla, then swirl in butter.

For pears: Preheat broiler. Line baking sheet with foil; lightly butter foil. Peel pears. Halve lengthwise and remove cores. Immediately rub with lemon to prevent discoloration. Using sharp knife, score rounded sides of pears lengthwise; do not cut through. Arrange pears rounded side up on prepared sheet. Brush with melted butter. Sprinkle generously with sugar. Broil pears 4 inches from heat source until golden brown, about 5 minutes.

Spoon sauce onto dessert plates. Top with pears. Serve immediately.

Kumquat Jubilee

A great finale for an oriental dinner.

4 to 6 servings

1 cup water
½ cup sugar
1 cup unpeeled kumquats, seeded and thinly sliced
½ cup fresh tangerine juice or orange juice
1½ tablespoons butter, room temperature

2 teaspoons sugar
½ teaspoon cornstarch dissolved in 1 teaspoon water
2 tablespoons Grand Marnier
3 tablespoons brandy
1 pint rich vanilla ice cream.

Heat 1 cup water and ½ cup sugar in heavy medium saucepan over low heat, swirling pan occasionally, until sugar dissolves. Increase heat to medium-high. Stir in kumquats and cook 12 minutes. Cool kumquats to room temperature.

Add tangerine juice, butter, sugar and cornstarch. Return saucepan to medium-high heat and simmer until mixture is slightly thickened and liquid is transparent, about 2 minutes. Add Grand Marnier and cook 2 minutes. Warm brandy in small saucepan. Ignite and carefully pour over kumquats. Spoon ice cream into bowls. Top with kumquat mixture and serve.

Orange Sauce

Can also be served with fresh fruit.

Makes about 1½ cups

¼ cup (½ stick) butter, room temperature
¾ cup sugar
⅓ cup fresh orange juice
4 tablespoons water

1 tablespoon grated orange peel
1 egg
Vanilla ice cream
Fresh mint sprigs

Cream butter with sugar in medium saucepan. Blend in orange juice, 3 tablespoons water and orange peel. Stir over low heat until smooth and creamy, about 5 minutes. Beat egg with remaining 1 tablespoon water in small bowl until well blended. Add to mixture and stir until sauce thickens and coats back of spoon, about 15 minutes. Scoop ice cream into dessert bowls. Top with warm sauce, garnish with mint and serve.

Hot Orange Dessert Soup

Serve with crisp almond cookies, page 109.

6 servings

5 tablespoons sugar
3 tablespoons cornstarch
2 cups water
2 cups fresh orange juice (do not use frozen)

1 to 2 drops vanilla
Pulp of 2 oranges

Combine sugar and cornstarch in saucepan. Gradually add water and blend until smooth. Bring to boil over medium-high heat, stirring constantly until thickened. Mix in orange juice and vanilla and heat through but do not boil. Stir in pulp. Serve in small Chinese tea cups or coffee cups.

Chilled Almond Ivory

A unique and refreshing Chinese dessert.

4 servings

1 envelope unflavored gelatin
1½ cups water
½ cup evaporated milk
½ cup sugar

1 teaspoon almond extract
1 teaspoon vanilla
Canned mandarin orange segments and lichee nuts

Soften gelatin in ½ cup water. Heat remaining 1 cup water, milk and sugar to just below boiling point. Remove from heat. Stir in gelatin. Blend in almond extract and vanilla. Pour into small shallow baking dish and refrigerate until set. Cut into cubes. Spoon into bowls. Serve with mandarin orange segments and lichee nuts.

Tangerine Mousse

6 servings

Tangerine or orange segments
1 egg white
¼ cup sugar

1 envelope unflavored gelatin
¾ cup fresh tangerine juice
6 eggs, separated
½ cup sugar

1 tablespoon grated tangerine or orange peel
1 cup chilled whipping cream
¼ teaspoon salt

Prepare waxed paper collar for 4-cup soufflé dish. Brush tangerine segments with 1 egg white, then dip in ¼ cup sugar. Set garnish aside to dry.

Stir gelatin into 3 tablespoons juice in small bowl; set aside to soften. Using electric mixer, beat yolks with ½ cup sugar until pale. Beat in remaining juice. Transfer to double boiler set over simmering water. Stir until mixture coats back of spoon; do not allow to boil.

Remove yolk mixture from over hot water and stir in softened gelatin. Pour into large bowl. Add peel. Cool slightly. Whip cream until soft peaks form. Beat 6 whites with salt until stiff peaks form. Fold cream into yolk mixture. Gently fold in whites. Pour into prepared dish. Cover and refrigerate at least 8 hours or overnight. Remove waxed paper collar. Garnish with tangerine segments.

Lemon Ginger Ice Cream

Makes about 1 quart

2¼ cups half and half
Grated peel of 3 large lemons
¾ cup sugar
6 egg yolks, room temperature

¾ cup fresh lemon juice
½ cup finely chopped preserved ginger in syrup, drained

Combine half and half and lemon peel in heavy medium saucepan and bring to boil slowly over very low heat. Remove from heat, cover and set aside 10 minutes. Beat sugar with yolks in large bowl until pale yellow and mixture forms slowly dissolving ribbon when beaters are lifted. Strain half and half, discarding lemon peel. Slowly pour hot half and half over yolk mixture in thin steady stream, stirring constantly. Return mixture to saucepan. Place over low heat and cook, whisking constantly, until mixture is thick enough to coat back of wooden spoon; *do not boil or mixture will curdle* (if curdling occurs, immediately transfer mixture to blender and mix at high speed until smooth). Transfer to bowl. Set over bowl of ice water. Cool completely, covering surface with waxed paper to prevent skin from forming.

Stir lemon juice and ginger into cooled yolk mixture. Refrigerate until thoroughly chilled, at least 1 hour. Transfer mixture to ice cream freezer and process according to manufacturer's instructions. Turn into plastic container. Cover and freeze until ready to use. Let soften slightly before serving.

Ginger Custards

4 servings

2 cups milk
2 tablespoons finely grated fresh ginger
1 teaspoon grated lemon peel

1 egg, room temperature

6 egg yolks, room temperature
5 tablespoons sugar

1 tablespoon finely diced crystallized ginger

Preheat oven to 325°F. Generously butter four 6-ounce ramekins. Bring milk just to boil in heavy medium saucepan over medium heat. Remove from heat and stir in fresh ginger and lemon peel. Cook over low heat 3 minutes, stirring occasionally. Remove from heat, cover and steep 20 minutes. Strain milk, pressing on ginger and lemon with back of spoon.

Lightly whisk egg with yolks in large bowl. Whisk in sugar until just blended. Pour in 1 cup ginger-flavored milk in thin stream, whisking gently. Using wooden spoon, gradually stir in remaining milk. Strain into measuring cup. Skim foam from surface.

Place prepared ramekins in roasting pan. Pour custard mixture into ramekins. Skim foam from surfaces. Transfer to oven and add enough very hot water to roasting pan to come halfway up sides of ramekins. Set sheet of foil atop ramekins. Bake until tester or point of small thin-bladed knife inserted in centers comes out clean, about 25 minutes. Cook completely on racks. Cover and refrigerate at least 3 hours. (*Can be prepared 1 day ahead.*)

To serve, run thin-bladed flexible knife around edge of each custard. Tilt slightly to free from sides, then invert onto plates. Shake up and down once to release. Sprinkle crystallized ginger atop each. Let stand 10 minutes at room temperature before serving.

Vietnamese Coconut Flan

A small scoop of finely crushed ice traditionally is placed on top of each serving. Flan is best if prepared one day ahead so flavors can mellow.

4 to 6 servings

¼ cup water
3 tablespoons sugar

¾ cup milk
¾ cup coconut milk

6 tablespoons sugar
3 eggs, beaten to blend
1 teaspoon vanilla

Finely crushed ice (optional)

Combine water and 3 tablespoons sugar in 8-inch fluted flan mold. Place over high heat and cook until sugar is dissolved and mixture is light brown. Continue cooking, stirring constantly, until syrup is dark golden brown. Remove from heat (syrup will continue to cook) and rotate pan so bottom and sides are coated.

Bring water to boil in steamer. Whisk together milk, coconut milk, remaining sugar, eggs and vanilla in medium bowl. Pour through fine strainer into caramel-coated pan. Set pan in upper section of steamer and steam flan 10 minutes over high heat; *do not overcook*. Remove from steamer and let flan cool completely in pan. Cover and refrigerate overnight.

To serve, invert flan onto platter. Cut into wedges and garnish each serving with a small scoop of ice.

Flan can also be steamed in individual 4-inch fluted tart pans.

Thai Coconut Custard

6 servings

1 pound fresh taro root, peeled and cut into 1½-inch pieces

5 eggs
1½ cups sugar

1 7-ounce can unsweetened coconut milk

1 tablespoon vegetable oil
1 tablespoon minced red onion

Combine taro root and enough water to cover in large saucepan. Cover and cook until tender, about 30 minutes. Press taro root through food mill or ricer to mash. Set 2 cups aside; discard any remainder.

Preheat oven to 375°F. Using electric mixer, beat eggs in medium bowl until foamy, about 1 minute. Mix in sugar and coconut milk and stir until sugar dissolves. Blend in taro root. Pour into 9-inch pie plate. Bake until golden, about 35 minutes.

Heat oil in small saucepan over medium heat. Add onion and cook until softened, stirring occasionally, about 4 minutes. Spread minced onion over custard. Serve warm.

Thai Green Rice Cream (Kha Ya Khoo)

In Thailand, fresh, nutty-flavored Pandanus (screw-pine tree) leaves are used both for flavoring and coloring sweets. Extract of Pandanus can be substituted and is available here in Thai markets.

8 servings

4 eggs (room temperature), separated
⅛ teaspoon salt

3 cups coconut milk *or* 3 cups whole milk flavored with 1 teaspoon coconut extract
½ cup short-grain rice
½ cup sugar
½ teaspoon salt

4 drops extract of Pandanus (optional)
8 hollowed-out orange halves, edges trimmed decoratively (optional)
1 teaspoon toasted sesame seeds
Fresh mint leaves

Beat egg whites with ⅛ teaspoon salt in large bowl until stiff. Bring small amount of water to boil in large saucepan. Divide meringue into 8 even mounds. Transfer 4 meringues to large strainer. Holding strainer about 2 inches above boiling water, steam meringues until firm, 5 to 6 minutes. Repeat with remaining meringues.

Combine coconut milk, rice, sugar and ½ teaspoon salt in top of double boiler. Place over boiling water, cover and cook until rice is tender, stirring occasionally, about 30 minutes.

Beat egg yolks in large bowl until frothy. Blend 3 tablespoons hot rice mixture into yolks. Stir yolks back into pan. Add Pandanus extract. Cook until mixture is thick and creamy, stirring gently, about 5 minutes. Transfer to blender and mix until smooth. Pour rice cream into shallow serving dish or individual orange cups. Top with meringue. Sprinkle with toasted sesame seeds. Garnish with mint leaves. Serve rice cream warm or chilled.

Chinese Almond Cookies

Makes about 3½ dozen

Glaze
1 egg
½ teaspoon salt

Dough
2½ cups unbleached all purpose flour
1 teaspoon baking powder
1 teaspoon baking soda
Pinch of salt
1¼ cups sugar
1 egg
1 cup (8 ounces) lard (room temperature), cut into 6 pieces

40 blanched whole almonds

For glaze: Combine egg and salt in food processor work bowl and mix 2 seconds. Transfer to small bowl. Cover and refrigerate. Wipe out work bowl with paper towel.

For dough: Combine flour, baking powder, baking soda and salt in work bowl and mix 2 seconds. Transfer to small bowl and set aside. Add sugar and remaining egg to work bowl and mix 1 minute, stopping machine once to scrape down sides of bowl. Add lard and process 1 minute. Return flour mixture to work bowl and mix using on/off turns just until flour is incorporated; do not overprocess. Wrap dough in plastic and seal tightly. Refrigerate until firm, at least 20 minutes.

Position rack in center of oven and preheat to 325°F. Shape dough into tablespoon-size balls. Arrange on baking sheet. Flatten into 3-inch rounds, then make sure cookies are spaced 1½ inches apart. Brush tops with egg glaze. Place almond in center of each cookie. Bake until lightly browned, about 15 to 18 minutes. Transfer to rack and cool. Store in airtight container.

Ginger Spice Cookies

Makes about 16

½ cup (1 stick) butter, room temperature
½ cup powdered sugar
1¼ cups sifted all purpose flour
2 tablespoons minced crystallized ginger
¼ teaspoon cinnamon
¼ teaspoon freshly grated nutmeg
Pinch of salt

Cream butter with sugar in medium bowl. Mix in flour, ginger, cinnamon, nutmeg and salt. Gather dough into ball. Shape into 4-inch-long roll. Wrap in plastic. Freeze until firm.

Preheat oven to 400°F. Lightly butter baking sheet. Cut dough into slices about ¼ inch thick. Arrange on prepared sheet. Bake until lightly browned around edges, 8 to 10 minutes. Cool cookies completely.

Macadamia Nut Torte

12 servings

Cake

- 4 eggs, room temperature
- ¾ cup sugar
- 2 tablespoons all purpose flour
- 2½ teaspoons baking powder
- ½ teaspoon salt
- 1 cup lightly salted macadamia nuts

Filling

- 4 cups 1-inch cubes fresh pineapple (about 2¼ pounds)
- 1½ tablespoons fresh lime juice
- 2 teaspoons grated lime peel
- 1 cup sugar
- 2 tablespoons (¼ stick) unsalted butter
- 1 tablespoon cornstarch dissolved in 1 tablespoon cold water
- 1½ tablespoons dark rum
- ⅔ cup coarsely chopped lightly salted macadamia nuts
- 1 small pineapple, peeled

For cake: Preheat oven to 350°F. Line bottoms of two 8-inch round cake pans with parchment. Mix eggs and sugar in blender until smooth. Sift together flour, baking powder and salt. Add to blender and mix again. With machine running, drop macadamia nuts into blender and chop coarsely. Divide batter evenly between pans. Bake until springy to touch, about 12 minutes. Run knife around edge of cakes and invert onto racks; remove parchment paper. Cool completely.

For filling: Puree 4 cups pineapple, lime juice and peel in processor. Heat sugar and butter in heavy large saucepan over low heat. Stir until sugar turns golden brown, about 25 minutes. Add pineapple mixture. Simmer, stirring occasionally, until reduced to 2 cups, about 2 hours. Blend in cornstarch mixture. Stir until mixture thickens, about 1 minute. Cool completely. Mix in rum. (*Filling can be prepared 2 days ahead and refrigerated.*)

Place 1 cake layer on serving dish. Spread ⅓ of filling evenly over top. Add second layer. Smooth remaining filling over top and sides of cake. Press chopped macadamia nuts onto top and sides. (*Torte can be prepared several hours ahead to this point.*)

Remove eyes from pineapple. Slice pineapple ½ inch thick. Cut each slice into thirds and core. Just before serving, arrange pineapple slices decoratively around base of torte.

❧ Glossary

With the growing popularity of Asian cuisines, many cooks are eager to try tempting oriental dishes at home. If you are new to this kind of cooking, the following glossary will help familiarize you with common Asian ingredients.

Noodles

Cellophane noodles (bean threads): Long and with a milky transparency, these noodles (also called long rice or *saifun*) are made from mung bean starch rather than wheat flour. They are added to soups and stir-fried foods, and are great for stretching leftovers into a hearty one-dish meal. Wrap tightly for best storage.

Rice sticks: These thin, semi-opaque noodles, known as *mai fun* in China and *sen mee* in Thailand, are formed from ground rice. The sticks may be presoaked or boiled for use in soups and snacks, or deep-fried to garnish a combination dish. They are sold in bundles and will last indefinitely if kept well wrapped in a dry place.

Udon: Originating in southern Japan, white *udon* noodles are made from flour, salt and water, and may be flat or round. Many stores sell dried udon, which have a long shelf life if kept sealed. Most Japanese markets also sell fresh udon, which may be refrigerated up to two weeks or frozen. Udon can be served in a simple broth or combined with pieces of vegetables, fish, poultry and/or meat for a more substantial meal.

Mushrooms and Other Fungi

Dried black Chinese mushrooms: Available in varying size and shade. Look for medium-size mushrooms with thick caps, as they provide the best flavor and fragrance. Soaking in hot water for 30 minutes restores the original size and texture; the soaking water is often added to the recipe for more flavor. Store tightly covered, as these mushrooms are susceptible to insect infestation.

Cloud ears: This dried fungus is very popular in Asian cooking. Thin and brittle, cloud ears become pliable after rehydration; though they have little flavor, their crisp texture complements many dishes. Keep cloud ears in a tightly covered jar.

Enoki mushrooms: With slender stems and tiny round caps, these miniature white mushrooms are often sold in bunches. Fresh enoki can be purchased in many areas and are preferred over canned; they can be refrigerated for a week. Enoki have a mild flavor, supplying crispness and a subtle aroma to soups, one-dish meals and salads.

Shiitake mushrooms: Shiitake are plentiful and versatile, making them a frequently used ingredient. The fresh mushrooms add visual appeal, texture and aroma to any meal. Dried shiitake are sold in several forms: whole, sliced, broken and as crumbs. (As with other dried fungi, the soaking water can be used in soups and sauces.) The fresh and dried have comparable flavoring qualities, and either can be added to combination dishes successfully.

Straw mushrooms: Usually canned, these smooth, small mushrooms with pointed caps add textural variation to any dish. Unused mushrooms should be rinsed and refrigerated in a covered container; they can be stored this way up to one week.

Spices and Seasonings

Dried shrimp: Usually added as a seasoning accent, dried shrimp have a concentrated, somewhat salty flavor. Buy bright pink shrimp that are curved, measuring approximately one inch from head to tail. They may be rehydrated in water or Sherry, depending on use. Dried shrimp are sold in plastic packages and will last indefinitely if placed in a sealed bag or jar.

Five-spice powder: Usually blended of ground anise, Szechwan pepper, fennel, cloves and cinnamon, five-spice powder is a pungent seasoning popular in Chinese meat and poultry dishes. Store in a tightly covered jar.

Lemongrass: A tropical grass widely used in Thai, Malaysian and Vietnamese cooking. The lower portion of the stalk, resembling a scallion, is chopped or cut to release a delicate lemony aroma. If fresh lemongrass is unavailable, the dried form may be rehydrated and used with excellent results. One teaspoon of powdered lemongrass, two strips of fresh lemon peel or a teaspoon of grated lemon peel are acceptable substitutes for one stalk of the fresh, though lemon peel cannot duplicate the herb's unique perfume.

Star anise: This often appears in Chinese dishes; it is used mostly with moist-cooked meat, poultry, game and fish. The distinctively star-shaped pods are often sold in plastic bags, and unused pieces should be transferred to a tightly covered jar.

Szechwan peppercorns: These tiny dried berries add a mildly hot flavor and piquant aroma to cooked, marinated and cured foods. They can be purchased seeded or whole; the seeded offer optimum taste. Some recipes call for peppercorns to be used as sold, while others recommend roasting and crushing before use. Stored in a tightly closed jar, they will keep indefinitely.

Wasabi (green horseradish root): *Wasabi* is a popular accompaniment to Japanese raw fish dishes such as sushi and sashimi. A small dab is usually sufficient, as it is intensely hot. Although the fresh form is rarely found outside Japan, most oriental markets feature powdered wasabi in tins and a paste form in tubes; refrigerate the paste after opening.

Pastes

Hom har jeung (Chinese shrimp paste): Grayish-pink in color, this sauce has a salty, strong shrimp flavor. It is often included in dishes with pork, fish, chicken, tofu, vegetables and fried rice, as its pungent aroma mellows when cooked (and sugar may be added to balance the taste if necessary). *Hom har jeung* keeps indefinitely in the refrigerator.

Kapee (Thai shrimp paste; also known as *trassi* in Indonesia, *bagoong* in Malaysia and *mam rouc* in Vietnam): A flavorful addition to Southeast Asian foods, shrimp paste is used in dishes from soups and sauces to condiments and grains. It is sold both fresh and dried. The fresh is pink; opened bottles should be refrigerated. The dried form varies in color from pink to gray and must be cooked prior to use. It is sold in cans and cakes, and can be stored for several months in a cool dry place if well sealed. Both forms are very aromatic, although the strong odor dissipates in cooking. Anchovy paste can be used as a substitute; use one-fourth the amount specified for fresh shrimp paste or one-half as much as the dried.

Miso (fermented soybean paste): Protein-rich *miso* adds flavor and body to soups and sauces. There are three forms of miso, each with distinctive coloring, flavoring and thickening characteristics. *Shiro* is white, somewhat sweet and thin; *chu* is golden, mildly flavored and with a medium consistency; and *aka* is red, intensely flavored and thick. Miso is sold in plastic containers, tubes, jars and bags and will keep up to one year if refrigerated.

Oriental sesame paste: Fragrant and flavorful, sesame paste is a popular dressing ingredient for cold vegetables and meats. Packed in jars and covered with oil, the hard paste is diluted with hot oil or water until creamy. Peanut butter thinned with a bit of oriental sesame oil may be used as a substitute.

Liquid Flavorings

Hoisin sauce: Creamy and reddish-brown, hoisin sauce is a mixture of soybeans, flour, sugar, salt, garlic and chili peppers. It adds sheen and sweetness to cooked dishes and doubles as a dipping sauce for seafood and poultry. Hoisin can be purchased in cans and will keep indefinitely if refrigerated in a covered jar.

Mirin (syrupy rice wine): Although technically a wine, *mirin* is used for cooking rather than drinking. Its alcohol burns off when heated, giving a mild sweetness and light glaze to grilled foods. If mirin is unavailable, prepare a substitute by heating equal amounts of saké and sugar. Stir constantly until the sugar has dissolved and the liquid is reduced by half.

Nam pla (Thai fish sauce): *Nam pla* is the liquid byproduct of fermented fish or shrimp. It is thin, salty and a translucent brown, and often serves as the base for other sauces. Practically ubiquitous in Thai cooking, nam pla is widely considered the best of the Asian fish sauces. Store opened bottles in the refrigerator.

Nuoc mam: (Vietnamese fish sauce): Prepared from fermented anchovies and salt, *nuoc mam* is so basic to Vietnamese cooking that it is called for in almost all recipes. The fermentation process includes three drainings, with the first yielding a light, clear sauce often reserved for table use. The sauce from the other drainings is of lower quality and is thus more commonly used in cooking. The term *nhi* on the label indicates a higher quality. *Nam pla* (Thai fish sauce) may be substituted, and like the Thai product, Vietnamese fish sauce should be refrigerated.

Oriental sesame oil: Pressed from roasted sesame seeds, this thick brown oil imparts a delicious nutty flavor and fragrance. It is packed in tins and bottles; refrigerate after opening to prevent rancidity. Do not substitute the light-colored, mild American sesame oil, which is neutral in flavor.

Oyster sauce: Ground oysters, soy sauce and brine combine to produce this thick, brown Cantonese sauce. Whether served as a dipping sauce or used as a seasoning for meat and seafood, oyster sauce enhances the natural flavors of other foods rather than imparting a flavor of its own. It is available in bottles and cans, and will stay fresh indefinitely if tightly covered.

Rice vinegar: Both the Chinese and Japanese produce a mellow rice vinegar used in cooking. The Chinese *chenkong* is black and can also be used as a dipping sauce. A mild red wine vinegar may be substituted, although the flavor of the finished dish will be slightly different. The delicate Japanese *su* is lighter and sweeter than Western products. Cider vinegar, diluted with a small amount of water or sweetened with a little sugar, can be used in place of *su*—but again, the imitation will not be quite as good as the original. *Sushi su* is seasoned Japanese vinegar, intended chiefly for use on sushi rice. It should only be used when specifically called for in a recipe.

Saké (Japanese rice wine): Aromatic and colorless, *saké* is a white wine with a dual purpose: It adds an intriguing sweetness while tenderizing meats, making it a primary ingredient in Japanese cooking. When warmed, saké is also popular as a beverage.

Soy sauce: Indispensable to oriental cooking, soy sauce is produced by fermenting soybeans, salt and wheat. There are several variations of this seasoning, each with distinct characteristics. *Chinese light (or thin)* soy sauce has a delicate flavor and is clear brown in color. The *Chinese dark (or black)* type is a thicker sauce, adding a rich sheen to foods cooked with it. Japanese *koi-kuchi shoyu* has a deep color and is used extensively in sauces and marinades; *usu-kuchi shoyu* is lighter, thinner and saltier.

Check the recipe carefully for the type of soy sauce specified. Try to avoid substitutions, as the Chinese products are generally more pungent, saltier, and thicker than Japanese brands.

Many supermarkets and specialty stores now stock Asian foods. If you cannot locate a particular item in your area, however, mail order services may be helpful. At press time the following stores offered many of the ingredients listed in this book. Please note that we are not endorsing the products or services offered, but merely providing a reference for your convenience. Check with each store for current price and availability.

Asia Food Products
3604 S. Grand Blvd.
St. Louis, MO 63118

The Japan Food Corporation*
445 Kauffman Court
South San Francisco, CA 94080

Kam Man Food Products
200 Canal St.
New York, NY 10013

Katagiri Company
224 East 59th St.
New York, NY 10022

Mandarin Delight Market
1024 Stockton St.
San Francisco, CA 94108

Mikado Grocery
4709 Wisconsin Ave. NW
Washington, DC 20016

Rafu Bussan Company
326 East 2nd St.
Los Angeles, CA 90012

Star Market
3349 North Clark St.
Chicago, IL 60657

Vietnam House
242 Farmington Ave.
Hartford, CT 06105

Wing Chong Lung Co.
922 S. San Pedro St.
Los Angeles, CA 90015

Yoshinoya
36 Prospect St.
Cambridge, MA 02139

Contact for a list of sources in your area.

Index

Credits and Acknowledgments

The following people contributed the recipes included in this book:

Barbara Adachi
Charles Allenson
Laura Lee Alpert
Sandi Anderson
Elizabeth Andoh
Angell's Bar & Grill, Boise, Idaho
Bob Arganbright
Joan Baxley
Susan Beegel
Lionel Bell
Terry Bell
Natalie Berkowitz
Jennifer Brennan
Patricia Brooks
Hugh Carpenter
Diana Cavey
Chan Dara, Hollywood, California
Ginger Chang
Norma Chern
Cheryl Clairardin
Dragon Inn, Overland Park, Kansas
Jane Salzfass Freiman
Grace Ann Gaskill
Cora Gemil
Phyllis Gorenstein
The Green Lake Grill, Seattle,
    Washington
Lyn Heller
The House of Hong, Honolulu, Hawaii
Larry Jacobs
Joy Garden, New York, New York
Kamolmal, Tarzana, California
Barbara Karoff
Lynne Kasper
Martin Kaye
Marlene Kellner
Keo's Thai Cuisine, Honolulu, Hawaii
King Tsin, Honolulu, Hawaii
Kon Tiki, Sheraton Waikiki,
    Honolulu, Hawaii
Kona Ranch House,
    Kailua-Kona, Hawaii

Alma Lach
Judith Lebson
Faye Levy
Madame Wu's Garden,
    Santa Monica, California
Mandarin Garden,
    Braintree, Massachusetts
Abby Mandel
Copeland Marks
Janet McMillan
Jefferson Morgan
Jinx Morgan
Dick Murphy
Bach Ngo
Elise Pascoe
Peng's Restaurant, Yonkers, New York
Thelma Pressman
*The Restaurant at Windows on the
    World,* World Trade Center,
    New York, New York
Bernard Rothman
Elizabeth Rozin
Prayad Saiwichian
Saladalley, Philadelphia, Pennsylvania
Richard Sax
Elizabeth Schneider
Shoji's, Portland, Oregon
Miriam Sinclair
Susan Slack
Shirley Slater
Karyn Taylor
The Thai Room, Chicago, Illinois
Trader Vic's, San Francisco, California
May Wong Trent
Pat Turner
Michele Urvater
Carol Lee Veitch
Joseph Venezia
Maggie Waldron
Jan Weimer
Gloria Zimmerman

Additional text was supplied by:
Hugh Carpenter, *Seven Steps to the
    Perfect Chinese Stir-Fry;* and Elizabeth
    Andoh, *Japan at Your Table.*

The Knapp Press
is a wholly owned subsidiary of
KNAPP COMMUNICATIONS CORPORATION.

Composition by Publisher's Typography

This book is set in Sabon, a face designed by Jan Teischold in 1967 and based on early fonts
engraved by Garamond and Granjon.